Educators in Action

EXAMINING STRATEGIC IMPROVEMENT EFFORTS

APQC®

PUBLICATIONS

American Productivity & Quality Center
123 North Post Oak Lane, Third floor
Houston, TX 77024

Edited by Paige Leavitt
Designed by Fred Bobovnyk Jr

Manufactured in the United States of America

ISBN 1-932546-26-X

American Productivity & Quality Center
Web site address: www.apqc.org/pubs

Table of Contents

Editor's Preface

This book captures success stories and important lessons from districts and campuses across the nation that are making a concerted effort to initiate real and sustainable change. The educators in these ten, in-depth examples have taken a systematic approach to improving student achievement, and readers will find some important common themes throughout the book. Like hundreds of campuses across the nation, these schools have adapted principles from the plan-do-check-act instructional cycle and its popular, derivative eight-step process.

Many of the schools have embraced this approach based on the successes of one district, detailed in APQC's book *Closing the Achievement Gap: No Excuses* by Gerald Anderson and Patricia Davenport. The story of Texas' Brazosport Independent School District is one in which students from impoverished and ethnically diverse backgrounds perform up to par with students from wealthier backgrounds, all due to an adjusted mindset in process improvement.

In the 1990s Brazosport faced tremendous obstacles in bringing disadvantaged subgroups of students up to speed with the district's better-performing students. In identifying ways in which to close this achievement gap, Brazosport educators studied approaches to continuous improvement from the corporate world. They met with business leaders in the Brazosport community to learn how they tackled the issue of improvement in their own work.

Within the decade, student performance had increased across the board—regardless of race, gender, or social condition—to some of the best scores in the state. The dropout rate declined from 6 percent to one-tenth of one percent, and the school district received the 1998 Texas Quality Award, an honor typically given to businesses. In addition, the district was named a finalist in the education category of the 1999 Malcolm Baldrige National Quality Award, and superintendent Anderson was named superintendent of the year by the Texas Association of School Boards/Texas Association of School Administrators.

The plan-do-check-act instructional cycle involves: making a plan spurred by valid and relevant data (plan); teaching on the basis of that plan (do); assessing the results of that instruction (check); and making adjustments to instructional practices based on follow-up data to then get even better results (act). Within the context of this approach and administered by educators who truly believe all students can learn, the eight steps are:

1. data disaggregation,
2. instructional timeline development,
3. instructional focus lessons,
4. assessment,
5. tutorials,
6. enrichment,
7. maintenance, and
8. monitoring process.

Closing the Achievement Gap: No Excuses provides an in-depth explanation of how the steps were applied at Brazosport and what were the results for that district. This book provides interesting examples of exactly how the process is adapted and how schools can make the eight-step process their own. This book is also compelling evidence that the process can work for any district or campus.

Each chapter in this book tells a unique story. Marion County Public Schools in Florida shares its first-year success with the eight-step process and how those initial gains are leading to additional support. Arizona's Crane Elementary School District, a K-8 district that has 6,000 students, improved its student achievement scores by implementing the eight-step process with limited assistance and funding. For the growing Gwinnett County Public Schools in Georgia, the eight-step process has been a tool to leverage finite resources to ensure students from different backgrounds all achieve educational success. With more than 70 schools and 43,000 students, Saint Paul Public Schools provided a strategic plan for improvement, developed with extensive school and community input, that inspired each school to craft its own solution to meet its unique needs. Roswell Independent School District in New

Mexico leveraged the arrival of a new superintendent to institute an accountability program inspired by the eight-step process. Florida's Highlands County Schools shares some critical lessons learned from its challenges in attempting to gain support for a plan-do-check-act approach. The Penn-Harris-Madison School Corp. in Indiana, with 11 elementary schools, shares lessons and results three years into its effort to provide focused instruction. Fontana Unified School District shares the story of one school in its near-Los Angeles suburban community to reveal challenges and rewards at the campus level and how it is coordinated with the district overall. The racially and economically diverse Horry County School District in South Carolina has used an innovative combination of approaches to overcome challenges in standardized testing, early student learning, new-teacher training, and parent involvement. Finally, with the help of a regional education support center, Muscatine High School in Iowa has proven that, by changing its belief system, the eight-step process works with older students.

All of these schools aimed for a "no excuses" culture and will inspire other districts to make significant improvements by acting on the belief that all children can meet standards no matter what their circumstances. Writers Becki Hack, Peggy Newton, Lee Simmons, and Emma Skogstad provide for each chapter critical success factors, actual test results and other indicators of progress, who was involved in the effort and why, and challenges faced. Some chapters also include actual lessons used in the classrooms and specific measures of success. Districts, schools, and individual educators can take away valuable findings to adapt to their own classrooms. Most importantly, the chapters cite tangible results—be it increased graduation rates, improved student and faculty morale, improved achievement scores, increased post-secondary enrollment, increased community involvement and funding, etc.—that can help educators gain support to initiate real and sustainable improvements.

Chapter 1

Florida School District's First-year Continuous Improvement Teamwork Earns Top Grades

By Becki Hack

Change models often emphasize starting small with a "quick hit" to show short-term results. As in baseball, change initiatives need at least a solid base hit to advance the cause. But knocking it out of the park is even more impressive. That is what Marion County Public Schools did, not with any of its baseball teams, but instead with its leadership in raising student performance.

A host of talent, a dedicated team, and a vision of excellence transformed this 45-school district from a "below average" performer to a rookie of the year contender. In 2002 to 2003, its first year of implementing the eight-step process, the district knocked a third of its schools off the Florida's "C or below" report card list and raised its percentage of schools reporting an "A" or "B" from 50 percent to 85 percent.

Marion County in central Florida encompasses 1,652 square miles and approximately 272,000 people. With 40,000 students and 5,200 employees, the public schools district has 28 elementary schools, nine middle schools, and eight high schools.

In 2001 the Marion County school board and former Superintendent Jim Warford committed critical resources and implemented the district's new vision: leading the state in raising student performance. Teamwork and collaboration netted superior results across the district. Although the results from its first year's efforts were as positive as hoped, the school district learned something unexpected but vital in the process: Contrary to most everyone's belief, schools had not fully understood or taught the curriculum required by Sunshine State Standards, which are student achievement expectations defined by Florida's state board of education by subject area and grade level (and used as the basis for state assessment testing in mathematics, reading, writing, and in 2004, science). The continuous improvement process changed that. This enlightening discovery as well as the district's resounding success instigated more positive change, even beyond its boundaries.

Warford has taken Marion County's vision to a statewide level, where he currently serves as Florida's K-12 chancellor and reported a successful 2003. That is, Florida's performance on the 2003 National Assessment of Education Progress (NAEP), otherwise known as "the nation's report card," led the nation in improving student achievement.

The Catalyst

It all began with a passion for improvement and a belief that all children can learn. Prior to his Marion County Public Schools tenure, Warford studied several improvement programs but became most interested in the eight-step process that Texas' Brazosport Independent School District created to achieve dramatic increases in student achievement. Once elected as Marion County's superintendent, he reviewed school test scores and determined that performance was, at best, below average. Determined to make a difference, he and the school board members committed to a continuous improvement process.

The process is based on the Brazosport approach. Its eight steps are:
1. data disaggregation,
2. instructional timeline development,
3. instructional focus lessons,
4. assessment,
5. tutorials,
6. enrichment,
7. maintenance, and
8. monitoring.

Warford and board members believed in the value of proven strategies and expertise of former Brazosport Superintendent Gerald Anderson. The school board's support was critical to not only the model's rigorous and rewarding first year in existence, but also its ongoing success. The board recognized the problem, offered help, listened to suggestions, established a new vision, committed resources through both personnel and funds, and aligned strategic objectives with the district's vision. The board committed funding to pay substitute teachers who were needed to fill in for teachers attending continuous improvement model meetings and training. And despite criticism and close scrutiny from the county's leading newspaper, the board set aside consulting fee funds for Anderson's assistance.

The new vision had teeth. To emphasize and measure the continuous improvement model, the board made student performance one of the district's ten strategic goals. In its 2002 to 2005 strategic plan and 2002 to 2003 annual objectives, the district lists three objectives within this performance goal.

1. For the first objective, the three-year goal is to increase the number of students in grades 3 through 10 achieving at level 3 (the minimum "passing" score out of five levels and defined as performance that "indicates that the student has partial success with the content of the Sunshine State Standards and correctly answers many of the questions but is generally less successful with the most challenging questions.") and above in reading and mathematics by 10 percentage points, as measured by the Florida Comprehensive Assessment Test (FCAT) in reading and mathematics. The annual objective is to increase those test results by 3 percentage points.

2. For the second objective, the three-year goal is to increase the number of students in grades 4, 8, and 10 achieving a score of 4.0 (on a scale of 1 to 6, with 6 as the highest score) and above in writing by 6 percentage points, as measured by the FCAT. The annual objective is to increase those test results by 2 percentage points.

3. For the third objective, the three-year objective is to collect, analyze, and develop performance measures based on 2002 to 2003 baseline data from FCAT science test results.

Implementation

Implementing the continuous improvement model was a true learning process for everyone. Marion County's team members launched the implementation plan in July 2001, when Anderson met with all district-level principals, all administrators, and key teachers to share the eight-step process. This launched the model.

The district's beginning leadership team was composed of the superintendent and three district-level administrators: former Director of Staff Development Diana Greene (who currently serves as the deputy superintendent of curriculum and instruction); Executive Director of Elementary Education Nancy Leonard; and Executive Director of Secondary Education Mary Lou Van Note. Warford charged this core team with preparing an overall plan with Anderson, which they began in October 2001 meetings. From this plan, Greene devised a training plan and materials.

Training began in January 2002 and targeted numerous district-level employees, as well as 250 school employees (five to six people per school) serving on each school's leadership team. Except schools for handicapped students (which do not take the FCAT) and charter schools (which had too few students or were too newly chartered to participate at the time), each preK-12 school was represented. (One charter school's board decided to opt into the initiative for the 2004 to 2005 school year.) The district team required each school to include on its leadership team at least one administrator; and it recommended to include at least one teacher from each grade level and a support person without classroom responsibilities (i.e., guidance counselor or specialist).

Due to logistical and training efficacy concerns, the large group was divided into two: elementary and secondary. With scheduling constraints, sessions were limited to one- to two-day blocks of time. Between January and June 2002, Anderson provided intermittent training sessions concerning the eight-step process, which totaled six days per group. He also provided one-day sessions concerning quality tools for the district team, who then served as trainers concerning quality tools for school leadership teams.

At Anderson's training conclusion, the district leadership team found they had more work to do. "We ended up with 250 people knowing how Texas did it, but not how to go back and train their own schools," said Greene. "It was naïve for me to think that these teams could just get up and leave and go implement at their schools." And they faced the reality of time shortage: only two days remained in their allotted training time for that school year. Thus, each group had one day to truly learn to apply the process.

Spurred into action, the district team took the information shared by Anderson, put it in a format to which Marion County schools could relate, and designed a complete training package schools could use to train their staffs. This "train the trainer" package included notebooks, training notes, PowerPoint presentations, handouts, and activities—and even scripts. (Other half-day training sessions were scheduled throughout the upcoming year to cover topics, such as Total Quality Management, that were important but not critical for teachers to know when beginning continuous improvement process training.) After their June training completion, teachers had the summer to meet and practice with their leadership teams prior to launching their own continuous improvement process training in August, on the first in-service day.

Concurrent to the training path in the district's compressed continuous improvement process rollout was a similar preparation path for assessments. Marion County encountered a bump in this road. Everything was happening so fast, district staff chose to concentrate primarily on training. Assessments were not developed, and the district staff felt that additional time was needed to develop assessment items for the frequent assessments. Not so, advised Anderson and Patricia Davenport, educational consultant and former Brazosport director of curriculum and instruction; instead, Greene said they recommended district staff "jump in and start the process" or else lose valuable time (many assessments and calendars would be needed by August 2002, a time when school staff would just begin training of all teachers). Thus, with the pressure on from February until August 2002, the district team began tackling what they soon discovered was a mammoth task: assessments, a critical part of the eight-step process.

The assessments Brazosport had purchased did not meet Florida's standards. "Every Florida school is provided an item specification for each tested benchmark detailing the type of test FCAT is, what is tested, and what is being assessed," said Greene. "We compared this item specification with Texas standards and realized we would have to write our own assessments." Van Note, Leonard, and their staffs took the helm at this point and gave Coordinator for Instructional Technology Debbie Mueller charge to design assessments.

Mueller, who said her title should be coordinator for curriculum alignment to more clearly portray her district role, spent the summer intensely researching and analyzing the FCAT item specification book and leading the district's assessment-writing process. Serving as quality control and writer, she worked with one full-time teacher-on-assignment (a role for former teachers, specializing in different subjects such as math or reading who were fresh from classrooms and still paid under the instructional salary schedule) and occasional assistance from groups of teachers to craft two assessments for each benchmark on the state assessment: form A for the first-time assessments and form B for those, following remediation, that would take the assessment again.

Writing all the assessments raised another issue. The Brazosport model calls for teachers to write their calendars, teach, and then assess. That was adjusted at Marion County, at least in the short term. "If we had to write assessments, we had to be in control of the calendar, because we could not let a school teach a benchmark for which we had not written an assessment," said Greene. "It really was done so that if we had not written the assessment, we would know when it occurred, and thus by what date to have it written."

Consequently, the district leadership team took control over the up-front work to ensure timely implementation of the eight-step process. The team wrote the initial 90-day calendar for schools, which were responsible for making calendars for every teacher, with an August deadline: by the first day of school, teachers would have the process, training, and calendar showing the skills to be taught in a specified order. (The district set the order to begin with weakest skills.) For the district leadership's initial effort, which Greene called "purely one of survival," the team received tremendous pressure.

In the beginning, the district office's role was very large; teachers had a limited role; principals' roles were not clearly defined; the process was top-down; the trust level was very low; people felt threatened; students were not successful; and there was no process point person. The problems were widespread. Principals felt unsupported. Teachers wanted more ownership of calendars and deeper explanation of assessments; they thought assessments were too difficult. Teachers did not like beginning the year teaching the most difficult skills; and they strongly disliked the 10-minute instructional focus from the Texas model, finding it too short on time. Not surprisingly, because 80 percent failed the first assessment, students hated the continuous improvement process. And the local paper took notice, placing the blame at the curriculum development office's doorstep. Marion County's continuous improvement process implementation had reached a critical breaking point: a breakdown or breakthrough? A determined and prepared leadership team took action.

From the outset, the district leadership team's core members and staff prepared to closely monitor implementation. For this, staff and curriculum development used their coordinators and teachers-on-assignment. The larger team's goal was to randomly visit schools, observe difficulties teachers experienced, talk with principals, offer assistance, and report back to the district. Schools would also contact the district. In addition, using its Total Quality Management training, the district leadership team went to schools and facilitated feedback sessions on the primary roadblocks.

At the top of roadblocks list were ownership of the calendar, longer instructional focus lessons, and a better understanding of assessments. The district team created a matrix of concerns, prioritized them, and began systematically dealing with the issues. This critical skill of monitoring and making adjustments made the difference. Greene said, "Schools were so happy. They felt like we were listening and responding to their needs. It was at this point that [the model] took off."

School Ownership

Attuned to schools' legitimate concerns, the district team relinquished ownership as soon as feasible. After the first 90-day calendar and lesson plan schedule dictated by the district, schools began developing their own calendars and the continuous improvement process took hold. Once it blazed the initial path necessary to survival, the district leadership team took the more advisory role it had envisioned at the outset. Gone was top-down control. In its place was consulting advice upon request.

Greene produced a calendar development video training and delivered it to her staff as well as one administrator at each school (usually an assistant principal); the administrator was then responsible for training other school staff, using the video if needed, to write their own calendars. Respecting school and teacher differences, the district team tossed out scripts and replaced them with interactive dialogue. District-level teachers-on-assignment, representing staff and curriculum development, were dispatched to struggling schools when needed to assist with calendar development. This guidance was not mandatory; schools decided if and when they needed help. Requests often came from teachers but occasionally from administrators concerned about consensus building. By October 2002 Greene had a full calendar scheduled to meet schools' requests for assistance to help develop the January to June 2003 calendar. Through November and December, district staff focused on calendar development and reassigned other duties where necessary. Eight teachers-on-assignment consulted with schools in pairs; doubling up bolstered facilitation strength and capacity.

Diverse needs require diverse treatment. Thus, said Greene, school ownership was the only answer. "They are the ones there every day. They know best what they need." This proved true the first year; with control now fully in schools' hands, Greene anticipated the trend to continue. Based on their respective schedules and staffing, schools make their own decisions on calendars, instruction, monitoring, tutoring, and enrichment. Each principal is accountable for his or her school's performance and is expected to seek the district's help when needed.

Teachers develop their own calendars as well as lesson plans, using a weekly collaboration period to review classroom activity and assessment results and discuss different teacher approaches. "They share information with each other to provide help," said Greene. "But, in the end, they use their own creativity and pedagogy to deliver the instruction." In some cases, several teachers may choose to deliver the same lesson across classes. No one is acting solo. Each third- through tenth-grade level per school is responsible for its calendar. Assessments, however, are still established at the district level to standardize testing across the district.

Assessments

Hard-won school buy-in and ownership would have been for naught had Marion County not invested in assessments. Faced with the daunting challenge of writing all assessments, Mueller worked with the district's existing model curriculum and assessment database to modify thousands of model test questions to meet FCAT's item-level specifications. Once she started delving into FCAT item specifications, Mueller discovered a specificity and complexity that rendered assessment writing difficult. FCAT requires real-world setting, specific formatting, no "none of the above" or "all of the above" questions, certain length reading passages, and other restrictions that limited Mueller's use of database questions. Seeking guidance from FCAT sample books marketed by companies as sample questions meeting Sunshine State Standards, Mueller faced another sad reality: contrary to their claims, most of those resources did not meet FCAT item specifications. Thus, the burden fell upon Mueller and those working with her to draft practice tests that met state benchmarks. Mueller said digging into the finer details of FCAT testing made everyone "better educators," as well as "better consumers and evaluators of the educational materials we use with our kids" because they truly understood what kids were being tested on and why off-the-shelf sample tests used in the past had not worked with expert teachers and hard-working students.

Mueller and those teachers willing to embrace this admittedly difficult task completed as many "mini-assessments" as time allowed by the new school year. They focused on those assessments that would be needed at school start-up and worked feverishly to continue writing assessments to meet the instructional focus calendar needs—often completing assessments only four or five days prior to their administration. This compressed schedule took its toll.

Total Quality Management feedback pinpointed the instructional focus and assessment as teachers' top frustration within the first six weeks. Teachers taught what they thought was the appropriate concept material but then found the assessments tested something altogether different. The district team and schools quickly learned that they had not fully understood FCAT's complexity. "We found out that no one really understood benchmarks as well as we thought we did," said Greene. "None of us really examined the benchmark in a way that we truly understood what was happening with the standards and what our kids were being tested on."

Again, Marion County had to tweak the Brazosport model. Whereas Texas standards could be taught in ten-minute instructional focus lessons, Sunshine State Standards could not. Concepts were complex, and students were unaccustomed to this type of assessment. (For example, they had never been tested on a 700-word reading passage, though that is what the state standard required.) Thus, the initial failing rate could be explained and overcome. The district leadership team then advised teachers to "teach to mastery" rather than limit focus lessons to 10 minutes: teach as long as students need to grasp the concept, but do not break the calendar. Redefining this responsibility eased teachers' fears that students would be unable to master concepts.

Yet another assessment hurdle arose in Marion County's rapid pace. Gaining a deeper understanding of FCAT standards and teaching to those standards was only part of the process; teachers also needed the ability to measure the impact of their work. The district discovered it had to fine-tune the Brazosport model not only for lesson plans, but also for detailed data analysis. Whereas Texas test data are reported broken down into lowest-level benchmarks, Florida FCAT data only breaks down by strand (i.e., one of the broad categories such as algebraic thinking or geometry, two of five categories tested in math)—not the benchmark within the strand. And data are broken down by school and grade but not by classroom. Thus, the leadership team had to surmount this challenge by creating its own mock version of the FCAT, called a "benchmark assessment," to administer annually, track results by benchmarks, and use data to make predictions and modifications to instructional calendars.

Greene said the benchmark assessment was a tremendous but valuable undertaking. Prior to its advent, schools used FCAT results to identify weak strands per grade and student and assume all benchmarks within those strands were weak. The district's new benchmark assessment distills data to the lowest level of detail, which allows teachers to truly identify weakest skills in their classrooms and then make the most effective adjustments.

Like with its mini-assessments, the district leadership team used ABACUS^{TM} software to create its benchmark assessments. Each school administers its test, uses its scanning equipment to grade tests, and owns and houses the results onsite. Although the district has mandated an annual benchmark assessment per school, it has not yet mandated a calendar. For 2004 to 2005, secondary schools have requested an April test date, whereas elementary schools want an August test date; Greene said the district will most likely set a November test date that will test what students have already learned in the school year but yet allow enough time to make adjustments for the weakest benchmarks.

The biggest challenge with benchmark assessments mirrors that of FCAT and mini-assessments: data. "I can't see any of the benchmark data because it is housed at individual school sites," said Greene. "What if there is a benchmark problem—say, 90 percent of our eighth grade students don't know a skill? That is a curriculum issue that needs to be addressed district wide." Thus, the district foresees a technology solution in the near future that enables easy access and decision making.

Team Players

As in the beginning, district and school leadership teams continue to interact regularly. The district's core team remained the same, with involvement of staff (such as teachers-on-assignment) as needed. What changed along the way was a clearer definition of roles and responsibilities, including the designation of a point person: a district team leader. Originally, the district team members shared leadership, with an individual taking the lead only when issues arose under his/her control. But with the first-round assessments' failing grades and local newspaper's finger of blame pointed at the curriculum department, the district leadership team appointed a more formal governance structure. Warford asked former Deputy Superintendent Jim Yancey to take the district team's helm. Later, upon Warford's departure, Yancey became superintendent, and Greene became the district's team leader and led the initiative's monthly, district-wide meetings. Schools know she is the point person to whom they direct questions, requests, and invitations to visit schools; they receive updates through a regular column in the school district's monthly newsletter. (Figure 1 depicts continuous improvement model team structure.)

In addition to the two original teams, several "vertical teams" were created to meet the schools' need for better data analysis. Each vertical team is composed of representatives of schools that flow in a developmental supply chain (e.g., six elementary schools and the middle school into which they feed, as well as the high school into which that middle school feeds). Representatives are typically administrators who each serve as point person for their respective schools. Executive Director of Staff Development Marilyn Underwood leads these vertical teams from the district level. Vertical teams arose as a result of the Total Quality Management feedback process; in surveying schools, the district team found data analysis, that all-important continuous improvement process step, to be the most important issue with which the schools were struggling and wanted help. Schools aspire to better understand what to do with their mountain of data: the continuous improvement process, benchmarks, and FCAT assessments. They want training and tools to help them use data more effectively. Underwood conducts monthly

CIM Team Structure

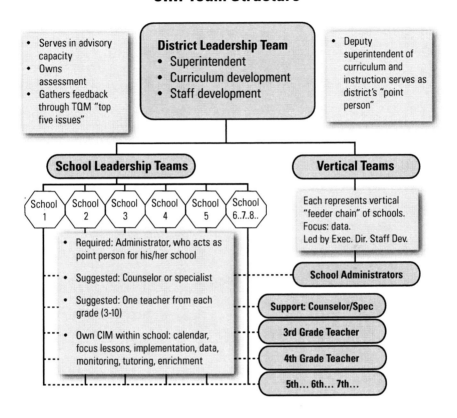

- Serves in advisory capacity
- Owns assessment
- Gathers feedback through TQM "top five issues"

District Leadership Team
- Superintendent
- Curriculum development
- Staff development

- Deputy superintendent of curriculum and instruction serves as district's "point person"

School Leadership Teams

School 1 School 2 School 3 School 4 School 5 School 6..7..8..

- Required: Administrator, who acts as point person for his/her school
- Suggested: Counselor or specialist
- Suggested: One teacher from each grade (3-10)
- Own CIM within school: calendar, focus lessons, implementation, data, monitoring, tutoring, enrichment

Vertical Teams

Each represents vertical "feeder chain" of schools. Focus: data. Led by Exec. Dir. Staff Dev.

School Administrators

Support: Counselor/Spec

3rd Grade Teacher

4th Grade Teacher

5th... 6th... 7th...

Figure 1

vertical team meetings, divided into feeder system teams, that serve as working training sessions to raise schools' comfort level with data.

Underwood meets regularly with Greene to exchange information and updates and ensure these teams are working smoothly. These data-focused meetings play an important part in overall progress. In Greene's monthly continuous improvement meetings that cover status, outlook, and additional training and communication needs, data issues continue to rise to the top, especially with Florida's recent science testing requirement. FCAT will now test science at grades 5, 8, and 10. Marion County is responding by asking its continuous improvement process and vertical teams to conspire and produce a pool of teachers to develop assessments that can be implemented in the 2004 to 2005 school year.

Greene's weekly meetings with executive directors keep her abreast of concerns. If problems appear significant, then she and her staff go out to schools and talk with the teachers. The district team gathers most feedback through the Total Quality Management process of identifying the primary issues. Teachers have identified data and monitoring as two important issues. In addition to forming vertical teams to address data, the district leadership team provided a "reminder" checklist: Do you have a fully developed calendar for August through May? Who is on your leadership team? How do you monitor your teachers? These and other questions guide teachers toward Marion County's common goals.

Principals count themselves as team players, too. They openly discuss issues with each other frequently and meet as a group monthly to share ideas and best practices. Through one such meeting, several high schools adopted a common format of preparing the continuous improvement schedule. The district also holds an annual best practices conference that district and school representatives attend.

Results

Prior to the continuous improvement process, all schools in the district were under-performing in the 2001 to 2002 school year. What a difference a year made. Of the 43 schools receiving report cards by year-end 2003, 15 broke through the "average" barrier and earned at least a "B" or better. (Florida's state grading scale designates 70 percent achievement as a "C," or "average," grade.) Eleven more schools than the previous year earned the coveted "A." And an impressive seven schools raised their grades by two letters: six jumped from "C" to "A," and one "D" school rocketed into the "B" category (Figure 2).

With such stellar achievement, the continuous improvement process is proudly displayed as part of the "Superintendent's Message" on the district's Web site; these pages highlight the eight-step process as well as Total Quality Management concepts. On this site, the district makes clear its commitment to improving student

	A	B	C	D	F	No Grade
Number of schools in 2001 to 2002	9	13	17	2	0	2
Number of schools in 2002 to 2003	20	17	6	0	0	0

Figure 2

performance. Under this model, it has set student mastery levels at 80 percent, which will require students to strive for excellence, not average results. The Web site publishes the district's position: "If we shoot for average, we'll only be average. If we shoot for excellence, our students will achieve excellence."

Although Greene said Marion County is pleased with its one-year success, she hastened to acknowledge more work remains. The district saw socioeconomic and racial gaps close slightly and will continue to improve this.

And more effort is being made to phase out the continuous improvement process as "this separate thing," Greene said. "It is what we do every day. It is good instructional practices."

When the local newspaper started raising questions about the effort—because they had heard no recent news and therefore assumed it had disappeared—the district had evidence the integration was working.

Marion County's results serve as a role model for others. Although Marion County does not own its assessments—technically, they belong to Pearson Digital Learning, which owns the question bank the district used to derive its modified test questions—the district worked with Pearson to benefit schools that most needed the best practices. All grade "F" Florida schools can write a grant for ABACUS student and curriculum management software; upon purchasing the software, these F-designated schools receive the assessments at no additional cost. It is more difficult to share calendar information because needs vary by school and classroom. Greene said that a school blindly using another's calendar without understanding the background and individual needs only sets up teachers and students for failure.

Rewards

Complying with the continuous improvement process is not an option for Marion County's 45 schools. That message is clear among school principals, whose performance appraisals include process-specific implementation and adherence questions. Greene is one of six who conduct these appraisals. She said principals know they are accountable, with job security hanging in the balance, for continuous improvement vigilance and progress. As leaders, however, their strongest driver is improvement. Thus, it only makes sense that schools own the rewards for their hard work. Although the district provides guidance and oversight, the individual schools, their teachers and administrators, and the students are in the trenches working doggedly to make a difference. The district monitors school compliance and helps celebrate these determined efforts; the state compensates those who accomplish the ultimate goal: superior performance.

The district leadership team encourages schools to build in celebration once every nine weeks for progress made on the instructional calendar and attends many of these school functions. But schools are the ones to make the ultimate decision on when and how to honor achievement. Some schools celebrate every nine weeks; others do not. (High schools, for instance, often have less of an emphasis on the model because the upper two grades are not involved with FCAT.) Many hold ceremonies at the beginning of the year in order to celebrate last year's scores and report card progress.

The Florida Department of Education, through its Florida School Recognition Program, provides public recognition and financial awards to schools that have sustained high student performance or schools that demonstrate substantial improvement in student performance. Greene said most Marion County schools received these "A+ awards" for their 2002 to 2003 performance, which amount to a sizable incentive at $100 per full-time-equivalent student. Additionally, Warford worked with a philanthropic organization to raise more than $100,000 that were awarded to the district schools with the highest, as well as most improved, achievement.

Technology

The district leadership team is currently scouring potential technology solutions to alleviate its greatest challenge: a mountain of paper and data that lack a common format. According to Greene, the current environment of copying, grading, and tracking assessments is a "paperwork nightmare." Benchmark assessments the district worked so diligently to produce provided results that were usable only at the school level; the district was unable to make sense of the data received from schools because they came by paper in a "plethora of formats." Greene said the SASIxp^{TM} software they are currently considering will alleviate this burden and allow schools to administer or record the assessments electronically and district personnel to efficiently access and sort the results. The district will purchase this technology for the 2004 to 2005 school year, input assessment data into a database, and make the tool available for school use by midyear.

As another important next step, the district hopes to replace its current student management system with a more flexible one and also offer Web-based tools—Pearson Digital Learning's ParentCONNECTxp® and Concert^{TM} Instruction & Assessment software—to schools, students, and parents to review student grades as well as FCAT and mini-assessment results. Although the district has made significant inroads in a short period of time, Greene said, "To be truly integrated, we need this technology piece."

Critical Success Factors

When asked what advice she would give others embarking on continuous improvement, Greene cited three critical success factors.

1. Believe that every child can learn. Greene said administrators and teachers must believe that from the start. But be prepared to support teachers and demonstrate how continuous improvement will work. Teachers may at first push back and doubt the process. That is what happened at Marion County; teachers had never seen assessments in the format or length provided by the district. "Leaders had to be there to support the teachers and help them understand why the assessments were developed the way they

were," said Greene. "This reinforces the need for training on the standards."

2. Training on the item specification book was provided to all Marion County teachers—not just math and language arts teachers. Every teacher is expected to support the reading and math calendar. For example, Greene said, physical education teachers can integrate math concepts by asking students to calculate mean and mode basketball scores. One district high school serves as a strong example of integration. It pairs social studies and language arts teachers to map lessons, and similarly its math and science teachers are grouped to integrate instruction.

3. Monitoring is the district role, according to Greene. "If you give a continuous improvement model to the schools and say, 'Do it,' don't expect it to move forward." The district must put a monitoring process in place with each school's administrative staff. At Marion County, once the daily ownership was transferred to the schools, the district had to follow up with an overarching calendar that informed staff of the timeline and due dates in order to avoid surprises. This provides ownership and accountability at the school level, while the strong guidance and leadership to enforce the process remains at the district level.

Marion County's toughest lesson learned was planning. Understanding the magnitude of the work and how the work would be accomplished was an eye-opening experience for the district leadership team. The team found the eight-step process is applicable in any state, but the resources used and how assessments are developed can differ significantly. In Marion County's case, according to Greene, the assessment piece was "huge." She said, "The eight-step process will work anywhere, but it is how you structure those eight steps that is key. My recommendation is to start slowly; make sure all your ducks are in a row before you start going out there quacking."

Starting slowly, however, does not necessarily mean rolling out with fewer schools. The key is knowing what is ahead—the scope of the job. By not understanding the scope at the outset, Greene said, the Marion County leadership team (especially those in the curriculum department rigorously preparing assessments) suffered "serious pain." Recounting that experience, she broached the possibility of a smaller rollout first to only the "D" and "F" schools, then immediately retracted the suggestion. "The results are so dramatic, how could we not have gone district wide? It all comes down to thoughtful, careful planning." She credited Marion County's talented staff, especially the three curriculum leaders, who worked under pressure to accomplish their tasks despite the almost insurmountable barriers.

The one-year results speak for themselves and underscore Marion County's most valuable lesson learned beyond implementation: truly understanding and teaching the state standards. Greene said the continuous improvement model "brought to light the true curriculum we were supposed to be teaching, and teachers now know what that is. It is the Sunshine State Standards."

It is obvious the students now know them, too. Some might say Marion County did not just knock the ball out of the park; indeed, it scored a grand slam.

Chapter 2

An Elementary District Takes Eight Steps to Quality Performance

By Peggy Newton

Many districts that face high levels of student poverty combined with limited resources become discouraged. How, they ask, can we overcome the chaos and uncertainty that students bring to class every day when our pockets are nearly empty from providing the bare necessities?

The Crane Elementary School District in Yuma, Ariz. has found an answer. It has significantly improved its student achievement scores by implementing the Brazosport model, which is based on Total Quality Management. And it has done so without the help of expensive outside resources. Crane prides itself on a "no excuses" culture and inspires other districts to make significant improvements by acting on its belief that all children can meet standards no matter what their circumstances.

Crane is a K-8 district that has 6,000 students in six elementary schools and two middle schools. The district is growing by approximately 5 percent each year and operates on a modified, year-round calendar. Four Yuma-area elementary districts, including Crane, feed into one high school district. The student body is 67 percent Hispanic and 25 percent white. The remaining 8 percent of the students are American Indian, Asian, or black. Sixty-seven percent of students are eligible for free or reduced-price lunches. The parents of approximately 20 percent of the students are migrant farm workers. Because of the harvesting season, the children of the migrant workers enroll in November and withdraw in early March.

The Crane district serves few affluent families, and its boundaries contain few businesses.

Learning About the Eight-step Process

The district calls its adaptation of the Brazosport model the "Crane Steps to Quality Performance" and refers to it informally as the eight-step process. The eight steps walk educators through a continuous cycle of improvement: planning, doing, checking, and acting. Crane has been involved in the eight-step process since 2000, when it realized that its students (especially children of migrant workers, second language learners, and Title I students) were not performing up to the state standards.

The project was envisioned in 1999, when Robert Klee was given the position of director of academic support. He became responsible for managing federal programs and overseeing testing. To prepare for his job, he attended a national conference in Texas, where he participated in a session conducted by the developers of the Brazosport model. After one-on-one time with the presenters, Klee returned with information for his management team composed of principals, assistant principals, and directors. He told them of his excitement and that he felt he had "been to the mountaintop."

In early 2000 Klee and two of his associates visited the Brazosport Independent School District, where he expected to find that the presenters had oversold their story. After an hour of observation, the visitors realized that Brazosport teachers were accomplishing even more than they claimed. Members of the Crane team believed that a similar initiative could help their schools.

"On the way back to Arizona," Klee said, "I had the feeling that I should apologize to every teacher and student that I ever supervised." He suddenly realized that he had sold them short, not expecting enough of them.

The district organized a summertime administrative retreat, which was held at one of the schools. Administrators began by studying the book *Creating the Total Quality Effective School* by Lawrence Lezotte (Effective Schools Products, 1992) and then built a training course so that teachers and principals would know and be able to work with the eight-step process. Administrators met with parents, teachers, and community leaders to set a new direction for the district. The district made a commitment: to make every child successful regardless of his or her circumstances at home. Every child would meet the state academic standards. The result was the enduring Crane district pledge, which states that all students will achieve the standards and that each educator is responsible that they do.

Before school began in 2001 administrators including Klee and Cindy Didway, the curriculum director, talked to their district's principals about the successful students in Brazosport and trained them extensively in the process. The principals were inspired and became true believers. However, their first attempt at implementing the process fell short, and Klee believes that the failure was due to lack of firsthand knowledge. "Because those involved had not seen Brazosport firsthand," said Klee, "they did not have the skills to pull it off."

In early spring 2001 the district sent the principals to Brazosport for two days to see the process in action. During their visit, the principals and administrators met in the evenings to discuss what they had seen and how they envisioned bringing it to Crane. Once the principals had visited Brazosport, their enthusiasm was renewed and they understood what they had to do.

Didway—who oversees curriculum, career ladder, and professional development—had been on the trip and believed it was necessary to also send the staff development team. She said that the staff development team had to internalize the concept that "every child can learn." Two months after the principals returned, the staff developers duplicated the trip to the Brazosport district.

According to Didway, the community has always considered Crane a good school district. "We felt like we were doing as well as we could with the kind of kids that we had." said Didway. "When we heard other school districts were doing better than we were, we chose not to believe it. The staff development team had to see for themselves." Klee said, "We decided to see for ourselves. That led us to Brazosport."

The Eight-step Process in Action

Since 2001, the district has examined each of the eight steps and implemented all it could within the limitations of its budgetary constraints.

Step 1: Disaggregating student data—Crane's performance is measured using the Arizona Instrument to Measure Standards (AIMS) test, which is the state's criterion reference test in reading, writing, and mathematics. Crane also uses the Stanford 9 (that is, the Stanford Achievement Test, Ninth Edition), which is a nationally normed reference test that measures adequate yearly progress (a requirement of the No Child Left Behind act).

The district has a data management office that tracks achievement and accountability requirements through the tests, and two staff members maintain the data. Assistant superintendents meet with principals before each school year begins to determine what types of information they will need. The data management office provides the principals with how individual students and different grade levels have performed historically. Principals are able to see how an individual student has been performing.

Data management is expensive, but it is a Crane priority. The district uses its 16-year-old modified "Zero" based budgeting process to help it spend its money where it will most affect performance, and administrators have identified data management as key to the success of the eight-step process. The district's lack of resources does come into play as it interprets its data. It cannot afford statisticians and analysts, but it does look carefully at what the data indicates.

In 1999, before the process was implemented, administrators aligned the curriculum and mapped it by quarters. They continue to work with the principals and teachers in collaborative teams. For example, a team may identify that last year's students did poorly on the "two-digit addition" math skill and adjust the schedule and curriculum to provide more support in this area. The disaggregation of scores leads principals to decisions regarding how to use their resources and what training to provide. The principals build their school budgets with the disaggregated data in mind.

Step 2: Developing instructional timelines—The next step is
the development of instructional timelines based on the priorities
that the data indicate. Each year, teachers within a school determine
the pace of instruction based on two criteria: how successful their
team (grade 4 math teachers, grade 5 English teachers, etc.) were
at presenting the skill and how each group of students (migrants,
English language learners, males, etc.) performed during the
previous year on related skills. These factors may either increase or
decrease the time spent on a skill.

Step 3: Delivering instruction—The district believes that all
students learn better when they are actively engaged in the learning
process. Ideally, all students should be fully engaged and using each
minute of time to learn. Teachers should not ask one child to stand
and read while the others passively listen. Students, for example,
might respond as a chorus while teachers walk to different areas
of the room to ensure that no one is quiet. Teachers should have
students actively follow instructions such as "write this down" and
"look this up."

The Yuma PLAN (Professional Learning and Networking),
which is a collaborative effort among all of Yuma's school
districts, trains teachers to actively engage students. Currently, all
administrators and instructional facilitators are being trained, and
(during the 2004 to 2005 school year) the plan will be incorporated
into the classroom with the teachers.

Step 4: Assessing frequently—After the delivery of instruction,
students take a short assessment consisting of five to ten questions.
Each assessment is specific to a performance objective, such as "using
context to determine the meaning of a word." Sometimes, teachers
do not wait until they have completely finished teaching an objective
before they test. A teacher might teach a unit on long division and
then test the students midway to evaluate their level of mastery and
to determine further direction for instruction.

Until recently, teachers created their own assessments.
They asked administrators to standardize assessments across the
district because they recognized differences among their various

expectations. During the 2003 to 2004 school year, district committees comprised of one grade-level teacher from each school and content specialists have been meeting to accomplish the standardization of reading and math. The task is not yet finished but the completed assessments are on target and are being used.

Crane's lack of resources has slowed the work of standardizing assessments. The district cannot provide enough substitute teachers to allow the collaborative teams the time to meet as much as they would like.

Step 5: Tutorial—Teachers use the assessments to identify individuals for tutoring. They regroup students so children hear the explanations of skills from a different teacher than they did originally. Didway said that hearing about a single skill from two different teachers helps the student understand. "If kids do not learn the first time, we do not give up on them; we give it to them again. If they do not get it the second time, we give it to them a third time in a different framework. We intervene until they get it."

Tutoring occurs both at a dedicated time during school hours and after school. Didway said that students are not pulled from their regular classrooms for tutoring, because they may miss important information and fall further behind. Each campus dedicates between 40 and 60 minutes a day for tutoring, but setting aside time for tutorials has been difficult. "The different schools are at various stages of implementation," said Didway. "Much depends on the leadership and the instructional staff of the school. We are finding the work much more challenging in schools that have a large population of students performing below grade level."

Step 6: Enrichment—Of the eight steps, enrichment suffers due to the district's lack of funds. The district has no formal enrichment activities either before, during, or after school. Individual schools have incorporated activities during the tutorial time for students who do not need reteaching.

Step 7: Maintenance—The maintenance of skills is deliberate and is part of the regular instructional plan. In some of the district's schools, teachers document their maintenance activities on a calendar that is monitored by the principal. Year after year, several schools purchase the Excel Math K-6 Curriculum© as part of their skill maintenance programs. Although the schools have limited resources, they have found that the Excel program effectively maintains skills, and they willingly invest in it, said Klee.

Teachers weave maintenance into their "bell-work activities." They give students these assignments immediately upon their arrival in the classroom. The assignments consist of a few questions that settle students down and help them begin to focus them on the day's concepts.

Step 8: Monitoring—The first level of monitoring is the responsibility of the building principals. Klee said that during the past five years, the principals have stepped into the role of instructional leaders rather than operations managers. They ensure that curriculums are aligned and scores are disaggregated.

Both principals and district administrators engage in onsite classroom monitoring. When they visit, they are looking for specific attributes of the quality process. So that teachers will know specifically the criteria on which their rooms will be judged, principals distribute "walk through" checklists. Each principal has a slightly different form that reflects the needs of the individual school.

When administrators visit, they are looking for teachers who have the performance objectives posted and are teaching to them. They make sure that students understand what they should be learning and are focused on the objectives. Students should be actively engaged in reading, writing, or other activities. The information posted on the bulletin boards should excite the students, and the room should have adequate reading material available. The arrangement of the room should encourage student involvement, and the teacher should be standing and actively engaged with the students.

Principals and administrators visit classrooms together and discuss what they have observed in the hallway immediately after the visit. The administrators may coach the principals and help them develop their instructional leadership skills.

The principals follow up the visits by meeting with the teachers in a coaching environment to discuss their strengths and opportunities for improvement. Didway and Klee meet with the schools' leadership teams regularly to answer specific questions about the eight-step process.

Instilling Accountability into the Eight-step Process

The monitoring process serves not only to maintain the status quo, but also to foster the cycle of continuous improvement. Continuous improvement is documented through the scoreboard of the New Century Achievement Goals program. The program is an accountability monitoring process and has been in effect for more than three years. The superintendent, Gary Knox, developed it because he observed that teachers and administrators received one set of test scores (the Stanford 9) annually, and they either celebrated or mourned on that basis. He wanted his staff to be able to measure its success in short time intervals.

Using input from Arizona LEARNS (the assessment arm of Arizona's Department of Education) and WestEd (an organization that helps schools achieve), Knox identified 52 different objectives essential to successful schools. He created a scoring grid with a "0" baseline and with "5" representing the ideal target. He established a rubric for each of the four steps between zero and five. Although some schools may have been performing at a slightly higher level, he arbitrarily gave all schools a score of zero in all objectives to start. District leaders reviewed the objectives to make sure that they were important indicators of success.

The objectives fall into the five categories that follow.

1. **Student achievement** examines the academic performance of various groups of students. The concept behind the student achievement category is ensuring that all students achieve at least one year's growth in one year. One objective in this category states that students who are eligible for free and reduced lunches should perform the same on standardized math tests as other students. The scorecard measures the gap between the average standardized math test scores for students the two student

groups. Rubrics for this example are:

0= A gap of at least 25 percent exists between the two student groups.

1= The school has created an action plan to close the gap.

2= The discrepancy between the groups is 11 percent to 20 percent.

3= The discrepancy between the groups is 6 percent to 10 percent.

4= The discrepancy between the groups is 4 percent to 5 percent.

5= The discrepancy between the groups is 3 percent or less.

This section of the New Century Achievement Goals is possible only because the district implemented the first step of its eight-step process, the disaggregation of student data. Through the services of the data management office, teams can accomplish other objectives related to the student achievement of groups such as migrant students, English language learners, and special education students.

2. **Teacher practice** examines the objectives that teachers should be accomplishing. One is the extent to which teachers are using the assessment data they have to drive their instruction. Another examines how the schools have standardized the way that teachers grade written material. Yet another assesses how well teachers are using standards-based lesson plans.

3. **School leadership** concentrates on what the principal and assistant principal can do to facilitate teachers in meeting their objectives. School administrators are also measured on their willingness to tell the community the truth about their performance. Didway said that reporting scores, whether they be good or bad, help principals own their data and not make excuses. Rubrics for this example are:

0= File scores away, and give stock information to parents.

1= Give stock information to parents quickly, within a two-week period of time.

2= Report the aggregated data and how individual groups (migrants, English learners, etc.) are doing.

3= The principal reports both the aggregated and disaggregated data to the public once a year.

4= The principal reports comprehensive, reader-friendly results to the public two times a year.

5= The principal reports comprehensive, reader-friendly results to the public four times a year.

4. **Parental involvement** is a requirement for receiving Title I funds. This category measures the extent to which the district has been successful in partnering with the parents in their children's education.

5. **District efforts** analyzes how the district creates the expectation that every child can learn and how it uses the eight-step process to prioritize its budget.

On the first working day of each month at the end of the school day, the district holds an implementation panel hearing to assess presentations made by administrators from various schools. Process owners from the schools appear before the panel and say, for example, "We believe we have moved from a score of 2 to a score of 3 in a particular objective, and here is why." They then present evidence that they have made the improvement. The panel quizzes the presenter to validate the progress and potentially awards a certificate of achievement within the following month. Every year, the district management team ties incentive compensation to how well teachers and principals achieve the New Century Achievement Goals. Administrators in the district are paid, in part, for performance, and advancing through the stages is part of the administrator's evaluation.

The implementation panel changes from month to month but always includes a governing board member, the superintendent, a supervisor, a principal or assistant principal, and a district office director (from curriculum development, special education, etc). An entire wall in the district office is dedicated to posting where the various schools fall in regard to the 52 objectives.

"The New Century Achievement Goals are vital to the district because they keep everyone focused on the only thing that is important: student achievement," said Didway. "It is so easy for those of us who are administrators to become diverted by other demands like angry parents or a problem on the bus. But once a month, all attention turns to the implementation panel that drives home the only reason we are here."

A successful presentation to the implementation panel should be cause for a school to celebrate. So far, the schools have progressed 1,034 steps, which should have produced 1,034 celebrations. However, the superintendent doubts that the schools have had 34 celebrations. He and his team intend to increase the focus on celebrating, an activity that should include both teachers and administrators. "The process has become too business-like," according to Knox.

Challenges

Crane is well on the way to fully implementing the eight-step process. It is proficient in disaggregating and using data to create instructional calendars, as well as creating and using assessments. However, it faces two primary hurdles in addition to those that concern its high student poverty level and its transient population.

The first hurdle involves handling high faculty turnover. Approximately 25 percent of Crane's faculty turns over every year for two reasons: the district is located in a rural and isolated area that teachers move out of it to find different opportunities and many teachers are the spouses of border patrol officers or servicemen stationed at a nearby Marine base. These families transfer frequently. The district is willing to hire the spouses on one-year contracts rather than lose the benefit of their talent entirely.

The district is concerned with the level of turnover and in 2000 conducted a focus group with 12 new teachers. Administrators asked the new teachers what could be done to make their experience better. The feedback from the teachers led to the hiring of instructional coaches, one for each building, to provide on-campus coaching and mentoring for the teachers.

The district has a comprehensive professional development program to assist new teachers. The teachers' contract has six induction days set aside for training. The teachers use a few of the days before they enter the classroom and the remainder throughout the year. The teachers are indoctrinated in the Crane pledge, the eight-step process, and the New Century Achievement Goals.

The district requires teachers to take coursework to develop their teaching skills. In 1989 Northern Arizona University established a campus in Yuma, and Klee said that the university has increased the quality of teachers.

The district is one of 28 throughout the state known as a "career ladder" district. Through the career ladder program, the state gives teachers additional funds when they involve themselves in student achievement initiatives.

The second hurdle involves coordinating with teachers to ensure everyone is on the same page. Klee said that before the district adopted the eight steps, teachers watered down the curriculum in response to student underachievement. "Now, if you go to a third-grade classroom, you should expect to see students doing third-grade work."

Administrators monitor the pace of instruction to make sure that every objective is taught. They have implemented a new standards-based report card, because teachers who are required to grade students on a topic must teach it first. The report card helps teachers stay on track.

Results

AIMS and the Stanford 9 are an integral part of a state profile of schools known as "Arizona Learns." All Arizona schools are placed into one of five categories: excelling, high performing, performing, under-performing, or failing. Six of Crane's eight schools are labeled "performing," and two are labeled "high-performing" for the 2002 to 2003 school year (Figure 3).

With the exception of one school, all schools in the district would have been labeled "excelling" except that they did not have a

School	Arizona Learns Status	Annual Yearly Progress
Centennial Middle School	High performing	Not met
Crane Middle School	Performing	Not met
H.L. Suverkrup Elementary	Performing	Met
Pueblo Elementary	Performing	Met
Rancho Viejo* Elementary	Performing	Not met
Ronald Reagan Fundamental	High Performing	Met
Valley Horizon Elementary	Performing	Met

*_Rancho Viejo Elementary is a large school that has recently been divided into two smaller schools._

Figure 3

sufficient percentage of students at the top of the assessment tests. (One of the requirements of the score card is to have a segment of high-achieving students.)

Overall, the district's AIM scores show improvement from 2000 to 2003. Scores for grades 3 and 5 are detailed in Figure 4.

The demographics of the Crane Elementary School District changed dramatically during the last 15 years due to the increase of migrant workers' children. Knox believes that an outsider looking in would expect that achievement scores would have plummeted, but they have not. They are better than they were 15 years ago. Knox

Percentage Meeting or Exceeding Standards in Math	Spring 2000	Spring 2003
Grade 3	48	72
Grade 5	32	62
Percentage Meeting or Exceeding Standards in Reading	Spring 2000	Spring 2003
Grade 3	67	78
Grade 5	61	60
Percentage Meeting or Exceeding Standards in Writing	Spring 2000	Spring 2003
Grade 3	79	77
Grade 5	47	56

Figure 4

said, "We are dealing with kids for whom outsiders would say don't have a ghost of a chance at being successful at school; we are going beyond the standard and are at the edge of very high ratings."

Chapter 3

A Georgia District Closes the Achievement Gap Between Affluent and Poorer County Schools

By Lee Simmons

The story of Gwinnett County in Georgia is not unlike that of any number of places in America. Located near a large metropolitan city, it is a growing county that claims nearly 700,000 residents, with 1.2 million expected to call Gwinnett home over the next 20 years. As is the trend across the country, Gwinnett County's growth has introduced a wider diversity among its people. Increasingly, African Americans, Hispanics, and Asians account for a growing proportion of Gwinnett's population. The county's proximity to Atlanta (only 30 miles to the southeast) provides an ideal destination for people seeking new opportunities for family and work.

Such growth has had its impact, particularly among the county's 90 public schools. The rising diversity experienced over the past few years has challenged educators to find new methods for using finite resources. With new expectations set by the No Child Left Behind act, that challenge has only compounded.

"Change is always difficult," said Tricia Kennedy, executive director of curriculum and instruction at Gwinnett County Public Schools. Kennedy oversees all K-12 curriculum development and implementation, as well as instructional strategies.

For Kennedy and Gwinnett educators, the federally mandated standards represented nothing less than a call to action in closing the achievement gap between the best-performing students and disadvantaged students who performed poorly. Exactly how they would accomplish this was less clear. The district had already been focusing on continuous improvement and for years had used corporate models of improvement. Educators were constantly scrutinizing student achievement data for indicators of students' performance levels.

Throughout this process, Gwinnett school administrators kept returning to one key area of improvement: how to shorten the performance gaps within student populations. Gwinnett's minority student rolls have increased significantly over the last 10 years, making student achievement gaps among subgroups a critical issue for the district. As of September 2003, the district counted 50.6 percent white students; 21 percent African American; 15.7 percent Hispanic; and 9.7 percent Asian.

For the district, the question was how these students from different backgrounds can all achieve educational success.

The Brazosport Spark

"For many years we have incorporated some corporate models of improvement," Kennedy said. "A big part of that is the review of data, including indicators of level of performance. One area for improvement is [performance] gaps within student populations."

In looking for best practices it could use to shorten those gaps, the district came across the work of Gerald Anderson and Patricia Davenport, two educators who helped initiate notable achievement successes in the Brazosport Independent School District in Texas in the early 1990s.

Located south of Houston, Brazosport faced tremendous obstacles in bringing disadvantaged subgroups of students up to speed with the district's better-performing students. Anderson first came to the helm in 1991, immediately after recent test scores indicated that students attending schools in Clute and Freeport, both district schools with poorer populations, scored low compared with students in the wealthier Lake Jackson area. Parents wanted to know why this was the case.

In identifying ways in which to close this achievement gap, Anderson and Davenport studied business methods of continuous improvement. Nine years later, Brazosport ISD had literally experienced a 180-degree turnaround. Students in the poorer Freeport schools were performing up to par with students in the wealthier Lake Jackson schools, regardless of race, gender, or social condition. The dropout rate declined from 6 percent to one-tenth of one percent. Davenport and Anderson now consult with school districts across the country in order to share their story and how it might be leveraged by schools facing the very same challenges.

To Kennedy and her Gwinnett County colleagues, the Brazosport story represented a turning point in their own journey toward excellence. Every school in her district has adopted the Brazosport methodology at some level. "As we were beginning to drill down our data looking for best practices, we came across the work that was being done in Brazosport, and were really impressed with their statistics," she said.

Adopting the Approach

After a 2001 presentation made by Anderson to Gwinnett County school officials and a piloting of the program at several schools in 2002, the district hired both Davenport and Anderson in the summer of 2003 to help implement the eight-step process that worked in Brazosport. The process was based on research that examined key factors at work in student bodies that were 90 percent minority, 90 percent poverty level, and at 90 percent proficiency in their targeted achievement.

The model "really centers around using data, frequent assessments, and collaboration to address a student's needs," Kennedy said. "… A recommendation came from a cross-functional action team that was reviewing gaps in achievement for the district among student groups. The team analyzed current achievement data and identified gaps, then looked to research-based models for closing the gaps and increasing student achievement. The eight-step process that originated in the Brazosport Independent School District was found to contain all of the most essential factors that research and practice shows impact student achievement and successfully close gaps."

Instead of adopting the model outright, Gwinnett schools took time to make their own changes that fit their circumstances. Pagie Ryals, principal of Hopkins Elementary, recalled that task as initially daunting. "We essentially took that model and tweaked it to call it our own," Ryals said. "For the first time, it came down to where teachers were looking at data, making lessons focused on that data, and targeting areas based on standardized testing where students were suffering in a certain area."

The district molded its approach on the following eight-step process:
1. data disaggregation,
2. develop an instructional timeline,
3. instructional focus,
4. assessment,
5. tutorials,
6. enrichment,
7. maintenance, and
8. monitoring.

The first component of the process, data disaggregation, calls for an overall look into present student achievement scores and how those compare across the district and nationally. All schools have access to an online database of reports on current student achievement data. Reports are available at the district, area cluster, school, classroom, and student levels, said Kennedy. All reports are also disaggregated by ethnicity, special education status, gifted education status, and economically disadvantaged. Reports for each standardized assessment include the weakest to strongest areas of performance, by subject and topic domain, the percentage and number of students in each performance level, and trend analyses of performance across years.

Based on that initial review, the next step in the model is to develop an instructional timeline. As long as they have appropriate time for instruction, said Kennedy, all students can learn. The timeline is developed each year by teachers based on their student achievement data, with more time devoted to subject areas that need the most improvement. The district provides a model timeline/

calendar for schools to use, based on district level data, said Kennedy. Schools may start with these timelines and tweak them to align with their school data.

Calendars are reviewed at the school and grade level as often as the assessments are given, Kennedy added. Teachers may decide after giving an assessment that additional time is needed for instruction on a standard and adjust the calendar accordingly. Most schools also review the calendars at the end of each grading period and adjust based on student achievement during that period. Once standardized assessment data becomes available, all calendars are reviewed and adjusted for the upcoming year.

Teachers have a hands-on approach to calendar development. The principal at Meadowcreek Elementary School and Meadowcreek third-grade teacher Crystal Collins, who was appointed committee chairperson for calendar development, approved a $20,000 budget to enable five teachers, one from each grade level, to convene for four weeks during the summer of 2003 to develop a new calendar for the school. Each grade-level representative was responsible for writing a year's worth of language arts and math mini-lessons for all teachers in his or her respective grade. Collins made sure the content was aligned with the district Georgia standards and signed off on each calendar with the principal.

Collins and her colleagues learned that students performed better in math than in language arts. Because Monday typically had the highest incidence of absence among students, the committee decided that teachers should teach math mini-lessons on Monday and Tuesday of each week. Language arts, in which students performed less well, were to be taught on Wednesday and Thursday when more children would be attending. Assessments were reserved for Fridays. Results from a Friday assessment test would determine whether a student needed enrichment or tutoring on a certain standard. So far, this process of instruction, dubbed the academic knowledge and skills/continuous quality improvement model, has seen some success among English language learners, which comprise 78 percent of the school population, said Collins.

This led to the third step of the instructional process, providing an instructional focus to target areas of weakness, typically in the form of a brief, direct lesson that teachers provide to students on a particular objective.

During the 2002 to 2003 school year, the Criterion-Referenced Competency Test (CRCT) is administered across Georgia in grades 1 through 8. Language arts, reading, and math are tested for grades 1 and 2. Social studies and science are added in grades 3 through 8. The test is given in a multiple choice format, is directly aligned to the state curriculum standards, and serves as Georgia's measure for AYP. That year, the test was rendered null due to errors in the administered test. Because teachers had no hard and fast results to look at, the faculty at Collins' school wrote and administered a mock CRCT based on Georgia educational standards to assess student performance.

"We discovered some things were not aligned correctly," said Crystal Collins, a third-grade teacher at Meadowcreek. "We were not getting to all the objectives."

In response, during the fall, after the committee compiled a calendar, it provided lessons and assessments to be used during the following spring semester, said Collins. Every teacher received a notebook containing mini-lessons and assessments for every week of the fall semester.

The fourth step involves assessments that focus on a targeted objective to determine whether students have learned the material. At Meadowcreek, first graders get a three-question, multiple-choice test every Friday; second and third graders get a five-question, multiple-choice test; fourth graders receive a five-question test plus one short-answer question; and fifth graders get a five-question multiple-choice test. "Many of these kids come in and have never seen standards assessments," she said. "They're able to see what the assessments look like before the tests come in. We can work very intensely on those objectives."

For those who still have not learned the standards, the process demands tutorial opportunities with a focus on immediacy in step five. Tutoring, said Kennedy, should happen immediately, rather than be put off until summer school. The sooner a student receives help, the better the chance of meeting a specified instructional objective.

"The tutoring, which we call Team Time, is built into the school day at the elementary and middle schools and at some high schools," she said. "Teachers team together to divide students by their assessment results—so that students who need additional help can be tutored in smaller groups and students who have learned the standard can receive reinforcement and enrichment—and divide themselves among the groups for the interventions and extensions."

At the high school level, some schools have built in time for tutoring during their lunch schedule. Students are assigned to teachers in the subject area where they need the most support, based on the results of their assessments. Other high schools provide before- or after-school targeted tutoring opportunities based on the assessments.

For students who meet objectives, enrichment opportunities (step six) are then provided so that students retain what they have learned. Such extensions provide enrichment to students who "get it" and are able to more fully grasp the standards.

The seventh component, maintenance, is a reminder that many critical objectives simply cannot be touched upon once and then forgotten for the rest of the school year. Retention is crucial, and those critical objectives must be returned to, however briefly, throughout the year.

Last but certainly not least, students and instructional leaders (i.e., principals, assistant principals, and teachers) must collaborate inside the classroom to monitor the process and identify areas of improvement. This includes ongoing checks of the instructional process, including frequent classroom visits by the principal, so that he or she can help teachers improve their instructional practices. It also involves frequent opportunities for teacher collaboration to share practices that are working.

All 90 Gwinnett County Public schools have implemented this process in some form since it was kicked off in 2002, including 23 high-poverty Title 1 schools in 2004. Before implementation, the district saw significant gaps between minority children who lived in poorer areas of the county and children attending the more affluent schools. The goal, said Kennedy, is simple: "We were simply looking for faster increases in student achievement within those subgroups."

Encouraging District Findings

Despite many initial challenges, Gwinnett County Public Schools has seen marked improvement in closing the achievement gap. One telling indicator has been student SAT scores, said Kennedy.

In 2003 the district's average student SAT score was 1036 (out of a possible 1600), and the average among African American students was 926 (Figure 5). (Eighty-eight percent of high school seniors took the most recent SAT. Although other students take the test, only seniors' scores are reported.) However, since 1998, the district has seen a 49-point increase for African Americans, compared to an overall 17-point increase during that same time for all students.

Kennedy and her colleagues have also found improvement in the number of subgroups participating and testing in advanced placement (AP) courses. The rigorous curriculum has proven successful for students from all socioeconomic backgrounds, which has prompted the district to encourage more students to enroll in AP courses. Since 1999, the district has seen a 120-percent rise in total AP tests taken. The number of African American students taking AP tests has risen 277 percent during the same period.

Building extra planning time into teachers' schedules seems to have made a difference in test results as well. In addition to teaching,

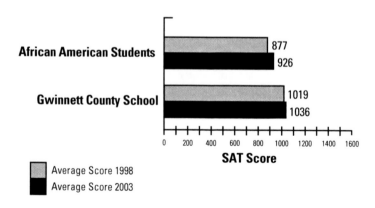

Gwinnett County Schools SAT Scores

Figure 5

Hopkins has implemented 40 minutes of planning time each day for teachers. When Ryals became principal last year, she had to hire half her staff because previous teachers had followed the former principal to a new school. It was critical to Ryals to train her colleagues quickly and infuse a planning slot into each instructional day, she said.

"It's caused the reality that they have to work together as a team," Ryals said. "Everybody is on the same page and talking in the same language about test scores and student achievement."

An Example School

Hopkins, a Title 1 school, uses the state's CRCT to help measure student achievement.

In 2003 Hopkins staff decided to compare test results with another low-poverty, middle-class elementary school to determine if they were meeting the benchmarks. The focus was placed on what percentage of students at both schools qualified as proficient or advanced in their reading and math scores. The results were encouraging to Ryals and the Hopkins staff. In reading, 93 percent of Hopkins' African American students scored within that category, compared with 73 percent at the wealthier school (Figure 6, page 44). For Hispanic children, the ratio was 80 percent to 60 percent; for white students, it was 100 percent to 93 percent; for students with disabilities, the ratio was 74 percent to 47 percent; and for students from economically disadvantaged backgrounds, the ratio was 84 percent to 67 percent.

The math scores were equally eye-opening, Ryals said. Ninety-three percent of Hopkins' African American students scored as proficient or advanced in math, compared to 62 percent at the other school (Figure 7). Ninety-five percent of white students scored as proficient or advanced in math, compared to 91 percent at the other school. For disabled students, the score was 68 percent, compared to 38 percent; and for economically disadvantaged students, the score was 81 percent, compared to 62 percent.

"It was interesting to see how well we fared compared to the other school," Ryals said. "It made the teachers feel good about how hard they had worked."

2003 CRCT Results
Reading

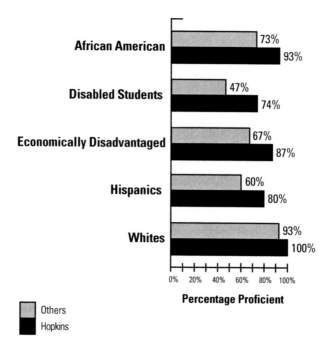

Figure 6

Success Factors

These early successes point to the fact that, when implemented properly, the process works. Success of any kind, said Kennedy, depends on the active participation of principals as instructional leaders. "Overall in general, it is the principals and their leadership that really make the difference."

Collins said that teacher buy-in has additionally become easier. "A lot of what we're hearing is, 'We're teaching to the test.' Well, the test is testing the objectives," Collins said. "Once our teachers understood that, they bought into the process much better. You can imagine a new program coming into your school. It's going to take you out of your element a little bit."

At Meadowcreek Elementary, all teachers were trained to use the new calendars that Collins and her committee had developed. The

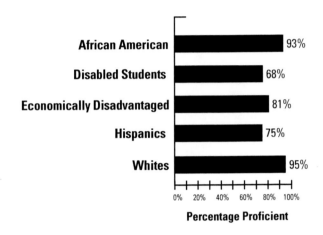

Hopkins 2003 CRCT Results
Math

Figure 7

committee continues to check in with every teacher on a monthly basis to make sure they are teaching the standards correctly.

A key to making collaboration between principals and teachers work lies in overcoming the traditional recognition of the principal as manager. Ideally, a principal serves as an instructional leader who works closely with teachers in identifying areas of improvement in the classroom, said Kennedy. Many of the district's Title 1 principals were early adopters of the eight-step process, she said, and those schools consequently showed some of the earliest gains.

"Principals have had to work with teachers to see the value of the effort in the time required to make this change," Kennedy said. "Teachers say they need more time. Because it is a collaborative process, it depends on teachers working together to share best practices."

That relationship lies at the heart of the eight-step process for Ryals and her colleagues at Hopkins Elementary, a K-5 and 1,196-student campus. Although they had always looked at test data to determine where to focus instructionally, Ryals said the new process redirected teachers and principals into thinking more about specific areas of need.

For instance, now teachers set aside up to 30 minutes every day to teach targeted lessons in language arts and math. The teachers then assess their classes once a week to see whether they have indeed grasped the concepts. Depending on those assessments, students are either placed into remediation or enrichment, Ryals said. Students move between interventions (tutoring/remediation) and extensions (enrichment) as their frequent assessments indicate their level of learning (every two to three weeks, in most cases).

Hopkins teachers adopted another important part of the Brazosport model: a weekly instructional focus, where they cover one specific skill every day. Although it is different from school to school, in general teachers at a grade level teaching a particular subject collaborate to develop and share brief lessons (10 to 15 minutes) on the standard that is calendared for that week.

Mini-lessons are teacher-directed (no independent worksheets), where the teacher explains, models, and guides practice. They are all delivered on grade level and involve all students, rather than just rote practice. Teachers incorporate high-level thinking skills and engaging activities just as they would for all parts of their instruction. The difference, said Kennedy, is that this time (that is, the "Target Time") gives an assured point of contact with students on the most critical and most difficult standards to be learned, and it gives additional instructional time on those standards.

These classroom devices have been bolstered by monitoring, said Ryals. Counselors and assistant principals regularly spend time with students from the different grade levels to look at where they stand in their instruction and what achievement goals they can set.

Process Critical Success Factors

To continue to implement the eight-step process, Gwinnett County schools will spend a considerable amount of time looking at changes in the way the process is scheduled. "The schedule is simply the framework around which the teachers are able to assure that they are doing those things that are most important to students' academic success," Kennedy said. "By building in the time to provide the targeted instruction; the time to frequently assess student learning; the time to provide the interventions and extensions; [and] the time to review and maintain skills and concepts, teachers know that they will be able to get that done."

One of the challenges has been to get teachers to come up with appropriate assessments for their students every two or three weeks. "There's never enough time in the day. They wish they had more time for planning and collaboration," she said. "This represents a change in the way teachers structure their day and their instruction."

Kennedy added that often when instructional time gets short, it is those very components that tend to "go by the wayside." By working together to build it into their daily schedule, teachers do not have to worry about whether or not they can make it happen, she said.

That and continuous training for teachers will determine continued successes. Ongoing training is already scheduled throughout the next year, Kennedy said, with a focus on emphasizing collaboration not only within schools, but also across schools. "Third-grade teachers at Hopkins Elementary need and want to know what third-grade teachers at Benefield Elementary are doing that is working with their students," said Kennedy. "The follow-up sessions will focus on that dialogue and collaboration. It is really critical in order to spread best practices."

Another key area for improvement is strategy. Using instructional strategies based on research has worked quite well in Gwinnett County classrooms so far. The eight-step process itself is simply a framework, Kennedy said. Solid, researched-based instructional strategies have to be used for the students to learn within that framework. "You have to have a process for instruction, but what you do with that instructional time is real critical," said Kennedy. "Using the strategies that research shows are the most effective is the missing piece to the puzzle."

The school district provides as many training opportunities to teachers as it can. In summer 2003 the district provided staff development for all 90 schools with Anderson and Davenport to conduct the training. The district has since followed up with three days of process checks held throughout the school year, as well as monthly leadership staff development meetings.

The district additionally provides ongoing courses on the eight-step process. Every spring, fall, and winter, teachers and staff leaders can sign up for district professional development courses. All schools have had the opportunity to send a leadership team to initial training in the eight-step process, Kennedy said. Davenport and Anderson personally trained these teams and plan to return summer 2004 to train teams in the nine new schools slated to open by 2005.

These leadership teams then return to their schools to work with and train the entire staff, and because they are colleagues and onsite, they can provide ongoing and timely training throughout the implementation process. In addition, the leadership teams have the opportunity for several follow-up sessions throughout the school year. At these sessions, they can discuss the challenges and successes of implementation with teams from other schools.

All administrators have 60 hours of training in the strategies and philosophy of continuous improvement, which provides the foundation they need to lead continuous improvement efforts at their schools.

Staff resources have additionally been developed by the district. An online lesson plan database allows teachers to submit tried-and-true lesson plans that are approved at the highest district levels. Since implementing the database, the district has provided modifications specifically designed for instructional focus ("target") time, assessment, tutorial, and enrichment times.

Teachers can submit their plans to the database, go through an approval process, and then make them available to every teacher in the district. An additional test generator database matches teacher-developed test items with the district's curriculum standards and is used to develop the mini-assessments that are a part of the eight-step process.

Successes in Implementing the Process

Although each school has had its own success story, Kennedy cites the successes at Hopkins Elementary as one of the shining examples of how process improvement has worked in Gwinnett County. Despite being a high-poverty school, the school showed significant increases in student achievement among their subgroups.

"When that school saw that their students were achieving at the same level as a school that doesn't have the same disadvantages among its population, but were also seeing that subgroups were scoring much higher, that was a real affirmation to those teachers," said Kennedy.

Teachers also report seeing improvement from using the results of the mini-assessments to determine the pace of instruction for each student, including whether he or she needs additional time or enrichment. Testimonials from teachers indicate that in the past they would have assumed all of their students were ready to move on after a period of instruction on a given standard; but they have readjusted their approaches based on data from the mini-assessments. "Whereas teachers reviewed student data in the past, this model has given them a process by which to use that data to determine the time devoted to instruction of the standards for each student," said Kennedy.

Teacher collaboration has also increased. Teachers have much more focused discussions about instruction with one another, because they have common calendars, common assessments, and common strategies to discuss. The best part about implementing the process, said Ryals, has been getting teachers onto a common wavelength regarding student achievement.

Although the school has come a long way in eliminating the gap among its subgroups, the challenge remains in keeping the momentum up. "Will it take time? Yes," Ryals said.

Still, teachers like Meadowcreek's Collins have already begun to see a difference in their students since implementing the process. Whereas students struggled to answer questions on tests that covered standards they had not covered before, students are now much more confident heading into the tests. "It's tremendously different from last year," Collins said. "Now, with the notebooks and built-in calendar, it's just wonderful. I definitely see the progress. This year, I knew they were getting it."

Chapter 4

An Uncommon Pair: Systemic Reform in a Site-based Environment

By Becki Hack

Saint Paul Public Schools' innovative leader transformed her urban school district by boldly expanding definitions and thinking regarding system-wide reform. Rather than impose the common approach to systemic reform, a "one-size-fits-all" mandate from the top, she turned the concept's traditional definition upside down and found a way to tailor custom solutions for individual schools while retaining district guidance. The district provided the overarching strategy, priorities, and support around seven broad objectives: implementing instructional best practices, offering more choice to students and families, partnering with families and communities, holding themselves accountable for continuous improvement, supporting leadership and professional growth, empowering schools and program sites, and embracing diversity. The schools were given the power, ownership, and authority to decide how to implement the district strategy to best meet their unique needs. To hear four district administrators, this "daring to be different" has changed their school district in a way that has already left a permanent imprint on students, parents, communities, staff, and future leaders.

Following Saint Paul Public Schools' exhaustive search and selection process, Patricia Harvey became its chief executive officer in 1999 and was tasked with providing instructional, organizational, and community-wide leadership. To better meet student and community needs, she embarked on organizational change. Working with a school board that was already convinced of the district's need to respond aggressively to public education changes, Harvey began decentralizing decision-making authority and responsibility to the site level by converting the district's single "school system" into what she calls a networked "system of schools."

Realizing that no two communities, schools, teachers, or students are exactly alike, Harvey did not expect one solution to solve individual issues across a district of more than 70 schools and 43,000 students. Instead of mandating a rigid, top-down solution, she envisioned a general framework—that is, a strategic plan developed with extensive school and community input—that inspired schools to craft solutions to meet their unique needs. She provided direction by focusing on 25 best practices firmly rooted in research, detailed in the district's action plan, and set schools free to blaze their own trails to those goals.

Pushing decisions down to those most familiar with their communities and the district exchanged bureaucratic control for truly empowered sites. Along with the newly expanded authority, Harvey gave schools the strong centralized support critical to effective school ownership: action plan priorities, best practices sharing, decision-making support and tools, professional development, quality reviews, and leadership development. Site-based planning, budgeting, results, quality, improvement, and accountability are all part of site-based processes, but they exist within the district's framework of systemic reform. Area C Superintendent Joann Knuth said, "This is an interesting marriage of two aspects of organizational reform that sometimes seem to be at odds, but here we have found a way to make them one."

By unleashing others' continuous improvement visions and creativity, Harvey has led Saint Paul Public Schools' compelling achievement over her five-year term: increased graduation rates, decreased drop-out rates, improved achievement scores, increased post-secondary enrollment, and increased community funding.

The Strategic Plan

Harvey, with school and community input, presented the strategic plan not long after her arrival in 1999. Part of the strong impetus was Saint Paul Public Schools' demand that it be a provider of choice. Executive Director of Strategic Planning Kent Pekel said the strategic plan was a powerful way of stating, "We will not become one of the cities in which the public schools are an option for those who don't have options."

The strategic plan provided the framework for Saint Paul Public Schools' success by outlining the overall continuous improvement direction that focuses on five target areas:
1. preparing all students for life,
2. providing clear and accurate reporting,
3. engaging the public,
4. creating institutional change, and
5. respecting and including cultures and differences.

If the strategic plan provided the frame, then the action plan, which followed two years later, painted the canvas in broad brush strokes. It mapped out the best practices for how schools would achieve the strategic plan's overarching goals. This collaborative effort among 1,500 educators, students, parents, community members, and others took place between January 2001 and January 2002, and it committed the school district to address the strategic plan's five target areas. Pekel said the action plan is a living document that is "instinctively rooted" in Harvey's leadership style—a leader he defines as a "relentless proponent of continuous improvement." Although Harvey expects the district to advance best practices and provide high-quality support of those best practices, Pekel said it is well understood that due to students' unique needs and the schools' better understanding of those needs, "It is rarely good for the district to mandate those best practices." He added, "This is a real difference from another pathway to systemic improvement."

As an example, Pekel pointed to other large school districts mandating literacy, math, and writing approaches and providing wide-scale training across often-immense teacher populations, which requires replicating implementation at every school site. Although that may simplify such issues as textbook purchases and professional development, Saint Paul Public Schools' approach advocates respecting each school's differences and existing best practices. Pekel said, "There is clearly a role for the district in promoting and maintaining a core level of quality," such as when school indicators are falling and the district needs to provide "everything from gentle support all the way to changes in leadership and staffing." But its primary role is to provide the framework and support for those best practices. That is why the action plan is so valuable.

The 2002 to 2005 action plan details 25 research-based core priorities within seven goals.

1. **Implement best practices in standards-based education**. Align curriculum, instruction, and assessment to high standards in order to continuously improve the achievement of all students while closing the achievement gap among racial and socioeconomic groups.

2. **Offer students and families a world of educational opportunities**. Implement a diverse array of high-quality programs, services, and other options to ensure that Saint Paul Public Schools are able to meet the unique educational needs of every student.

3. **Hold the district accountable for continuous improvement**. Develop, implement, and refine an accountability system that holds everyone involved in education responsible for results.

4. **Partner with families and the community**. Working together, the district will increase the percentage of families and community members who are actively engaged in helping students achieve high standards.

5. **Support leadership and professional growth**. Expand and improve leadership and professional development programs to engage all staff in high-quality opportunities for growth that are sustained, intensive, collaborative, and site-based.

6. **Empower school and program sites**. Further decentralize decision-making authority to the school and program level and strengthen the capacity of schools and programs to implement comprehensive school reform.

7. **Embrace diversity as one of the district's greatest strengths.**
   Strengthen the capacity of schools, programs, and central
   administration to understand and meet the educational needs
   of students, staff, and community members from diverse
   backgrounds.

"Essential efforts" further detail each of the action plan's seven
goals. For example, the first goal, implementing best practices in
standards-based education, comprises five essential efforts. The
first is to implement instructional best practices. This involves
implementing research-based, best-practice approaches to instruction
in the following core academic areas: creative arts, foreign language,
language arts, mathematics, science, and social studies. (The district's
priority best-practice instructional approaches for 2002 to 2005
are: balanced literacy, an educational strategy that blends language
and phonics instruction through guided and independent reading
and writing; integrated math, an educational strategy that engages
students in the interdisciplinary study of math—as opposed to the
traditional separation of algebra, geometry, and trigonometry; and
inquiry-based science, an educational strategy that promotes students
as scientists by experiencing hands-on exploration, observing
details, raising questions, using traditional science concepts to solve
real-world problems, communicating through various methods,
proposing solutions, and critiquing practices.) Other efforts for this
goal include reforming high schools, accelerating learning, expanding
school readiness, and developing demonstration schools.

"These are the things that research and experience tell us will be
the best for Saint Paul," said Pekel. The action plan articulates these
best practices and goals, but the district allows each school to define
the pathway best suited to individual needs, as long as the school is
continuously improving. Regardless of their direction and site-based
priorities, however, all schools are accountable for results.

Pekel said this approach avoids wasting time debating a top-
down mandate. And when one school shows tangible results from a
best practice it selected, other schools gravitate toward what works.
Pekel cited that district's Project For Academic Excellence as an
example. This comprehensive school reform initiative started in three

schools as an initial test, expanded to eight, and then grew to 11; now it encompasses most all elementary schools in the district.

With the advent of the No Child Left Behind act, the district adopted those federally mandated indicators as the primary measures of success. Although the district knew, from research and experience, that its action plan strategies would raise achievement on NCLB indicators, flexibility remained key. When a school is not investing in the action plan strategies but is making progress on the performance indicators, "that is absolutely fine," said Pekel. "In fact, we ought to be paying attention to what they are doing because we may want to reorient our efforts."

The converse is also true. If a school's indicators are heading in the wrong direction, then the first question is whether the school is investing in action plan strategies; if not, then the area superintendent works with the school principal to align strategies with those proving successful in other schools.

The Project for Academic Excellence is one instance where the district became more involved due to a common, district-wide problem. When indicators raised concerns that middle schools needed additional instructional support, the district interjected its guidance and aligned school strategies rather than allowing schools to continue down divergent paths in addressing the same problem. Pekel said, "Rather than throwing everything out and looking for new strategies, we look at core strategies that are working elsewhere in the district and attempt to adapt them."

The district has made important progress in reaching goals set in the strategic plan. Some of the biggest strides discussed by administrators follow.

- **Site-based decision making**
  - Collaborating at the school and program level (programs focus on a specialized area of study, such as engineering or liberal arts, and can exist separately or within a school) to develop a strategic continuous improvement plan that aligns with the overarching district action plan
  - Reorganizing the district's central administration to support site-based improvement

- Empowering school and program sites by creating and strengthening local decision-making "site councils," which are governing bodies comprising community, faculty, administration, students at high school level, and parent representatives
- **Data-based decision making and quality reviews**
  - Insisting on accountability for results
  - Increasing student achievement on local, state, and national assessments
- **Comprehensive school reform initiatives**
  - Focusing on research-based, best-practice approaches to instruction in core academic areas
  - Laying the groundwork for reinventing high schools through the Blueprint for Better High Schools
- **Leadership**
  - Developing a new generation of principals and other school leaders

Guiding its day-to-day action plan are seven "habits of mind" that the district has embraced in approaching challenges.

"1. We believe that all students can achieve to high standards.
2. We know that one size does not fit all.
3. We make decisions based upon research and evidence.
4. Our standard is continuous improvement, not perfection.
5. We are committed to collaboration in all that we do.
6. We believe diverse perspectives improve our work.
7. We recognize that continuous improvement requires shared leadership."

Site-based Decision Making

The school board and Harvey decentralized decision-making authority because they believed that the best decisions for children are those made closest to the sites. Whereas decisions for facilities maintenance, food services, and supplies are best made from a centralized standpoint, Executive Director of Leadership Development Dennis St. Sauver said personal choices like budgets and staffing are better made by the schools. Thus the goal was that each school establish a site council composed of its "community" representatives—parents, teachers, administrators, business partners, students at high school level, and sometimes family or community resource partners—to help shape and support the school's mission, participate in the development of the strategic continuous improvement plan, drive school change, have input into the selection of the school's principal and staff, and help plan and prioritize the school's budget.

Half of the district's schools had site councils in place before the strategic plan; but the new direction required all sites to establish a council—which they did by June 30, 2000. To effectively transfer decision-making authority, Saint Paul first had to organize, train, and empower people to take over site-based leadership. Thus, the district used a foundation grant to establish and train site councils for the 70 to 80 schools by training more than 1,200 site council members to serve on governance bodies for their respective school sites.

Harvey created a District Office for Site-Based Improvement to oversee these councils. Each site council is responsible for participating in annual strategic continuous improvement plan development, agreement, and submission to the superintendent. The strategic continuous improvement plan is aligned with district goals and addresses all school initiatives such as curriculum, technology needs, budget decisions, and hiring needs; major initiatives made at school sites are included in the strategic continuous improvement plan and go through the site council.

One of the important things from the beginning, said St. Sauver, is that site councils were actively involved in selecting their own building principals. In the three years site councils have been in place, 35 principals have been hired using the process. Although the district supplied the candidate pool through its Leadership Institute's rigorous qualification process, every school had a team composed of site council members who interviewed, screened, and selected three candidates whom they recommended to the area superintendent; in all but one instance, the superintendent made the final placement based on site council desires. "This has been a big change in terms of the way schools have been doing business," said St. Sauver. "They've been given authority, decision-making power, and—the key, I think—some major training we have provided for them."

Site councils typically range from 8 to 20 members, with an average size of 12, and are comprised of staff, parents, and community members such as business partners or family or community resource representatives. No more than half can be staff such as classroom teachers, support staff, or non-licensed staff. The only two required members are the principal and the teachers' union representative. Additionally, a district guideline requires councils to reflect the diversity of their schools.

Schools can decide whether to hold elections for their councils, which St. Sauver said schools choose if they have highly active parent involvement, or recruit and select volunteers. Where elections are held, candidates often prepare a biography and make presentations; staff vote for staff, and parents vote for parents. At less active sites, parents volunteer to fill openings. Typical terms are two to three years; some initial terms were shorter to avoid the burden of replacing an entire council. Councils meet monthly for two to three hours; subcommittees may meet additionally for such items as budgets or strategic continuous improvement plan preparation.

Building site council members' capacity to perform their role, though, must come first in order to enable effective site-based processes and decisions. That, acknowledged St. Sauver, takes some work. This entails structure, support, and education. The district sets standards and provides support, data, and accountability. Training has been the crux and, according to Pekel, critical from a quality perspective. Recounting the difficult lessons learned by other school districts that decentralized authority prior to building capacity, Pekel said where requisite skills or support were lacking, people retrenched and claimed decentralization was not working; and schools too hastily re-centralized rather than conclude they approached decentralization incorrectly. He said Harvey has witnessed this in prior experience and thus focused critical efforts on building the structure, support, and skills necessary at Saint Paul Public Schools.

At the outset, the district held large auditorium meetings for all people interested in learning more about the site council concept. Today, the central office provides most training to site council co-chairs, usually a parent and a teacher, who then share with the entire council. Site councils receive training on how to: build teams, plan and solve problems, run effective meetings, achieve diversity, and resolve conflict. The district takes it one step further by conducting an annual statewide conference on the topic of leadership and the site council. In the conference's four years, it has attracted between 300 and 350 attendees each year.

One of the greatest struggles for site councils, said Knuth, has been "coming to an equilibrium of decision making and final authority between the professional staff—particularly the principal—and the parents. We do have site councils that want to exert more power and authority and control than is appropriate to the process." The district has published and delivered clear guidelines, the terms of agreement under which site councils operate, to all site councils. Some councils have worked efficiently in the last four years, while others are grappling for the right decision-making balance. Ultimately, however, the expectation is that principals work collaboratively, gather input, and share decisions, but have the final authority and responsibility for site councils decisions.

Knuth says moving to a site-based environment contributed to a "wonderful reality:" a community that has passed two referendums in four years to increase the amount they pay to support Saint Paul Public Schools, which is something voters had not done in decades. Knuth said Harvey's leadership has created an environment where parents and the community are very much aware of schools. "Therefore, they came to the table to support us in a time of need."

Crucial to this empowerment is not only the training, but also the infrastructure. To facilitate the connection between the central office and schools, Saint Paul Public Schools established three "area superintendents," who are each responsible for 23 to 24 schools. Two additional area superintendent's are responsible for area learning centers, summer school, after-school programming, and community education and early childhood programs. Knuth, who serves as an area superintendent, says she works closely with the Office of Site-Based Management, principals, and site councils. She said the interaction between the district function and the schools has become customer-focused—"our customers being the schools."

To better serve its customers, the district trained central office staff to preemptively serve schools rather than forcing schools to seek out answers from the district. For example, a budget analyst and a human resources staffing specialist are assigned to a specific area and attend monthly area meetings to answer any of the schools' questions. The benefit of this, said Pekel, is central office staff's better understanding of individual school issues and comprehensive area priorities, rather than "just knowing one bureaucratic slice of the work." Principals have three district support people—budgeting, staffing, and communications—who are knowledgeable about the schools and the community and develop ownership of the schools within their area.

Data-based Decision Making

As part of its critical support role, the central Office of Accountability and Support Services provides schools the data, tools, and assistance they need to make better data-based decisions, which is an important part of the action plan. The Research, Evaluation, and Assessment (REA) department within the Office of Accountability and Support Services is responsible for:

- conducting regular student assessments and testing;
- coordinating and developing system-wide assessments and testing;
- reporting student progress;
- compiling data for school district advocacy at the state and federal levels;
- examining the progress of various educational programs used in the school district; and
- analyzing data for the school board, superintendent, and other district officials.

According to Research, Evaluation, and Assessment Director Tom Watkins, "At the district and school level, we really are relentless about accountability and improvement. We use the most meaningful measures available." That means ensuring measures are the most appropriate for the schools. In fact, said Watkins, Saint Paul and other active districts have helped shape the No Child Left Behind act measures.

When examining apples-to-apples comparisons (by matching students on poverty, ethnicity, English language learner and special education status), Saint Paul's students are performing at or above the Minnesota average, which is consistently one of the highest in the nation. Watkins said the district feels it has some good demonstrations of success. And although there are still "plenty of gains to be made in the coming years, we feel convinced that we are on to something here and that we've made tremendous strides," he said. "Each one of our groups has made tremendous gains; it is a matter of keeping it going and applying what we do know to a greater level of detail than we've ever done before."

Watkins pointed to test results as examples.

- **Minnesota Comprehensive Assessments**—reflects the state high standards for the purpose of the No Child Left Behind act. In the 2003 to 2004 school year, this included math and reading for grades 3, 5, and 7; reading for grade 10: math for grade 11; and writing for grades 5 and 10. The district uses these results to monitor its performance status. Since the test was first administered in 1998, student achievement has more than doubled. (Figure 8 illustrates the percentage change between 1999 and 2003 in grades 3 and 5.)
- **Minnesota Basic Skills Test**—measures individual performance against Minnesota's exit requirements in math and reading for grade 8 and written composition for grade 10; grade 12 students must pass all three tests for graduation eligibility. The number of students passing on the first attempt has increased since 1999, with impressive achievement in grade 10 writing (Figure 9).
- **Stanford Achievement Test, Tenth Edition (SAT10)**—measures individualized student achievement from year to year in grades 2 through 8. The school district uses the SAT10 to calculate cohort (longitudinal) achievement growth and to compare student performance against a nationwide sample of students in reading, math, social studies, and science. The district administered this new assessment for the first time in April of 2003 and is encouraged by the baseline results. All grade levels in social

Figure 8 – Minnesota Comprehensive Assessments
Percentage of students with "solid grade level skills" or better

	1999	2003	Change
Reading Grade 3	32%	52%	+23% points
Reading Grade 5	36%	62%	+26% points
Math Grade 3	32%	57%	+25% points
Math Grade 5	27%	56%	+29% points
Writing Grade 5	47%	54%	+7% points

Figure 9 – Minnesota Basic Skills Tests
Percentage of students passing on first attempt

	1999	2003	Change
Reading Grade 8	49%	56%	+7% points
Math Grade 8	44%	45%	+1% points
Writing Grade 10	63%	77%	+14% points

science and language, as well as two grade levels in science, are performing at or above the national average in the three grade levels tested. Whereas only two of the seven grades tested in math performed at or above the national average, the remainder came close (Figure 10, page 72). "There is room for growth, but these are encouraging signs," said Watkins. Language scores are particularly positive considering that 40 percent of the district's students do not speak English as their first language. In language and reading, the district plans to monitor growth in subtests such as reading comprehension and vocabulary to ensure it is connecting with English language learners.

These test data are available to schools online and can be cut and compared in numerous ways (e.g., state, district, school, and subgroups) for schools to assess and act on performance results. According to Pekel, the Research, Evaluation, and Assesssment department provides increasingly good summative data to schools,

Figure 10 – Stanford Achievement Test, 10th Edition (SAT10) for 2003

Percentage of students in average or above average range nationally (stanines 4 to 9)

National norm = 77%

	Grade						
	2	3	4	5	6	7	8
Reading	66	68	73	76			
Math	71	72	80	76	72	69	78
Language	*	*	71	*	89	*	79
Science	*	*	80	*	72	*	76
Social Science	*	*	77	*	77	*	79

* Not tested.

Note: Spring 2003 was a baseline year for the SAT10. Results cannot be compared directly to earlier test results from the Metropolitan Achievement Tests.

which must then engage in inquiry by assessing what is working and what is not concerning curriculum sequence, instructional method, needs of kids, etc. For those schools needing improvement, Knuth said one of two things usually happens: Schools more sophisticated and experienced with analyzing data typically begin targeting improvement areas and goals to include in the strategic continuous improvement plan, and schools less familiar with data analysis will receive help from the Research, Evaluation, and Assessment department and the area superintendent. Problem areas are identified, goals are established and included in the next year's continuous improvement plan, and adjustments are made to meet those goals. Adjustments are made when necessary at the classroom level. Partnering with the Research, Evaluation, and Assessment department, the Office of Instruction oversees continuous improvement in classroom assessments, data analysis, and focus lessons.

Watkins and the Research, Evaluation, and Assessment department work with schools to ensure the strategic continuous improvement plan goals have staff and site council buy-in and are reasonable and feasible by student group and subject area. "We want them to make growth that is at least in the average range for the district, if not in the above average range," said Watkins.

Technology tools are yet another way the Research, Evaluation, and Assessment department supports the schools. The research, evaluation, and assessment Web site provides district schools continuous access to a variety of reports such as school profiles, demographics, district test results, statewide results, and subgroup reports they can use on an ongoing basis. In addition, schools can use Swift Knowledge, which is a Web-based data analysis tool that connects all previous test data to each site's current enrollment. Whereas a grade 5 teacher may have been limited to pulling and sifting through hard copy data in the past, she/he can now create a quick electronic roster of an incoming class' prior test history. Watkins said use of Swift Knowledge is not 100 percent; but all principals and many school leaders have already attended training and taken advantage of the tool, and many are "at the point where they are able to use that data to effectively inform decision making."

Although it has been exciting to provide schools the data they need to highlight trends and determine what is working at individual sites, Pekel said the epiphanic moment will come when sites are able to identify the effective practices contributing to that trend. "I think that is where we are going to turn the corner on data-based decision making," said Pekel.

The district's Project for Academic Excellence embodies the data-based decision making set forth in the plan-do-check-act process. Although the district did not start with that definition, "Essentially what we have done is implement the process, and by design, it is very much a quality process," said Knuth. Schools not only receive the data from the Research, Evaluation, and Assessment department, but also receive data coaching. Watkins said this is a great opportunity to bring together key decision makers with the staff to carefully review and make sure everyone understands the data received. Once schools understand the data, the Research, Evaluation, and Assessment department helps them take action on the data by providing increasingly intensive levels of training in each curricular area of best practice. "It provides the 'how to' in delivering instruction," said Knuth. "REA is providing results to examine so we know how to put that quality circle in place: how to analyze, assess, and redesign."

Quality Reviews as Part of an Accountability Plan

The Office of Accountability is responsible for "quality reviews," which involve several observers visiting a site to administer surveys and conduct interviews to gain a better understanding of each school's conditions. Many issues center around climate and general satisfaction, and the evidence gathered is both quantitative and qualitative. Several central office staff representing multiple departments conduct these two- to three-day site visits and target 10 to 15 schools per year. Although the process is uniform enough to gather quality evidence, the process is sensitive to the school's given conditions. It includes candid feedback and significant input from parents and the community. "The quality review can go beyond what a traditional evaluation or accountability system would do because accountability systems take uniform measures across all sites, report on them, and come up with a summative report," said Watkins. "In the case of the quality review, it is much more sensitive to the goals that are operating within that site and can yield much more meaningful results."

Collaboratively, central office, teachers, principals, parents, and others have streamlined the school continuous improvement plan to focus much more on data, results, and revised objectives. "So now what needs to happen in the quality review, rather than taking a look at the general template for 'good schools'—a good beginning for us—the review will now shift and ask schools to analyze their own effectiveness in addressing the goals they have identified from their own data analysis," said Pekel.

For instance, if a school had identified a problem with a set of students, family involvement, or a particular instructional area, said Pekel, "The quality reviews will now be an impartial, external mirror to hold up and give that school a chance to self-assess its effectiveness in addressing those goals." The district anticipates this change in focus of quality reviews will occur in 2004.

The quality review outcome is a rather detailed report focusing on strategic areas such as leadership, academic success, and climate issues. The Office of Accountability shares the report with the area superintendent and the school principal, who then share it with the entire staff and site council to analyze and determine quantitative and qualitative goals to include in the continuous improvement planning process. The district plans to take each school through the process once every three years.

Although the quality review process provides a great learning opportunity for the central office, the district hopes it can soon comply with the action plan's goal of having school representatives conduct quality reviews at other district schools. Said Pekel, "This is wonderful professional development and sharing of best practices." Although some schools have started this with limited participation due to time constraints, the district aspires to reach this goal because of the value teachers and administrators receive. In that vein, the district has begun targeting emerging leaders, particularly at the assistant principal ranks, to become members of the quality review teams. This links leadership development to the review process.

Comprehensive School Reform Initiatives

Saint Paul Public Schools' comprehensive school reform took shape across its schools through two programs.

1. **Project for Academic Excellence**—an initiative introduced in 2002 to unify the direction for standards-based curricular instruction. It started in three schools and has since spread to most elementary and junior high/middle schools.

2. **Blueprint for Better High Schools**—an initiative launched in 2000 to reinvent high schools by creating small learning communities. All seven high schools have developed and begun implementation of their own vision of the Blueprint's goals.

Saint Paul Public Schools' Project for Academic Excellence, partnering with the Institute For Learning at the University of Pittsburgh to gain research-based knowledge and "principles of learning" guidance, began slowly in 2002 and 2003 by targeting schools who failed to make adequate yearly progress following academic probation and focusing on classroom best practices in balanced literacy, writer's workshop, integrated math, and inquiry science. The program's success attracted other schools; participation has rapidly grown to 53 schools. The goal is to offer all district children the highest-quality education—within a proven, standards-based framework—to better prepare them to face the future confidently, develop rewarding careers, serve their communities, and value learning.

The primary focus in reaching this goal is teacher training and support through the district's Professional Development Center for Academic Excellence. The Center provides ongoing training on the best standards-based practices in curriculum and instruction (particularly in reading, writing, math, and science), in-school support, and continuous feedback. It is a clearinghouse for instructional materials, curriculum guides, and documents to support district-wide initiatives. The center works with a select demonstration school to act as a model by offering hands-on training—a sequence of training, observation, and application—in developing best practices that teachers can use in the classroom; this initiative is beginning to spread across the district.

"The Project for Academic Excellence under-girds, really, the raising of the level of instruction and therefore the academic success of students in schools where it is implemented," said Knuth. "The district is providing the training for principals and teachers to assess the outcome of that increasingly effective instruction."

One powerful process that schools are undertaking in this initiative is curricular mapping. Schools have already shown results by aligning areas of instruction across each grade level by focusing first on reading and then math and, where applicable, implementing other subject areas or integrating the design of the school's magnet focus (e.g., arts, aerospace, humanities, and science and technology). If school sites choose to implement curricular maps, then they follow sequential steps in mapping each subject area: essential questions, goals to be reached, strategies to reach them, standards to be met in those strategies, and outcomes. The map becomes a living document available to all parents, staff, and other schools interested in benchmarking—a prevalent culture at Saint Paul Public Schools.

The Blueprint for Better High Schools arose out of Saint Paul Public Schools' desire to reinvent high schools to increase achievement scores, graduation rates, and college matriculation. The district wanted to better prepare students for future success. Leaders knew the purpose and structure of high school had to change so that all students, not just college bound students, would complete an educational program that helped them meet high academic standards. Although it had many high performers, the district faced:

- **a disturbing drop-out rate**—at least a third of the freshmen entering its high schools never earned a high school diploma,
- **large achievement gaps**—significant disparities existed and were growing in some cases among socioeconomic and racial groups, and
- **lagging English language learner and special education achievement**—achievement scores were behind district averages.

The district was aware of the odds stacked against it. Said Pekel, "High school improvement is a lot harder then improving elementary schools, at least according to the data." But with solid determination, it began engaging important stakeholders. It launched a year-long conversation with Saint Paul community members. Feedback showed people valued the advantages of large high schools—course offerings, facilities, and extracurricular activities—but they thought too many students were getting lost in the crowd. Using this information and research, the district narrowed its focus to small learning communities because overwhelming evidence shows that such communities increase graduation rates, improve attendance, boost completion of higher-level courses, and raise student achievement. It set and published its goal:

> *By our target date of 2004, every student in our seven large high schools will be a part of a small learning community that connects students to (1) a group of 300 to 600 peers and (2) at least one teacher or other adult who will provide consistent guidance and support throughout the student's high school career.*

Thus, small learning communities became a critical piece to the overarching goals, or "three Rs," of the Blueprint for Better High Schools.

1. **Rigor**—Every student is fully challenged. One of the measures of this, said Pekel, is making sure more students from all backgrounds are taking accelerated coursework like advanced

placement, International Baccalaureate™, or other such challenging curricula.

2. **Relevance**—The high school experience explicitly speaks to what students will do in higher education or the workplace. Pekel said the manifestations of this are significant increases in the students participating in internships, community service, and college planning. Starting in the 2004 to 2005 school year, the district will implement its "six-year plan" with all incoming high school freshmen; students will use a Web-based tool to map out their high school paths and at least two years of higher education.

3. **Relationships**—Students form close, caring relationships with their teachers and peers in order to increase students' interest in school, desire to meet their potential, and graduation rates. Small learning communities were created to fill this need and provide students those small-school connections along with their big-school opportunities.

True to its site-based decision making, the district left high schools free to structure the small learning communities in different ways. But it identified five core requirements, which reinforce the "three Rs," for all to meet.

1. **Set high standards**—Each community must help all students, not just those bound for four-year colleges and university, to reach high academic standards through rigorous coursework.

2. **Build relationships**—Each community must be organized to connect each student to at least one caring teacher or another adult who will provide guidance and support throughout the high school years.

3. **Connect school to future**—Each community must help all students develop goals and plans for life after high school by exposing them to the worlds of higher education and work through participation in post-secondary options programs, internships, career counseling, and other efforts.

4. **Promote professional collaboration**—Communities must also facilitate collaboration among teachers who work together to design curriculum, improve instruction, and address student needs.

5. **Provide opportunities for all**—Students and parents will choose their small learning communities. All communities must be open to all students with no requirements for admission other than enrollment at the larger high school. Along with small learning communities for all students, each high school will continue to offer a full menu of extracurricular activities and key school-wide programs, such as athletics, band, performing arts programs, world languages, advanced placement, and International Baccalaureate classes.

The central office role remains the same: articulate broad strategies and provide increasingly high-quality school support. This underscores the district's respect for existing high school successes and acknowledges that not all high schools need a "radical restructuring," said Pekel. Schools have varied in pace and approach in undertaking the blueprint. Whereas some schools are emphasizing small learning communities, others may focus on supporting students in taking more rigorous programs. Where to focus in the three Rs is a site-based decision.

The same flexibility is true with restructuring high schools into small learning communities. Within the district's guidelines, schools determine the structure, focus, size, and curricular approach. For instance, schools can structure schools-within-a-school, in which students take all or almost all of their classes in one of several small, separate, and autonomous schools within a larger school building. Or schools can set up "houses," in which students spend a significant part of their time learning with the same group of peers and teachers, while also taking other courses offered on a school-wide basis. (This model is analogous to the models used by universities and the "colleges," such as education or law, within those universities.) The third option is career academies, in which students take school-wide courses along with work-related classes in a specific field, such as information technology, finance, health sciences, liberal arts, engineering, and global visions (international affairs).

No matter the structure, every high school provides "advisories" as part of the blueprint program. Within the smaller learning community, an advisory is designed to give students time (e.g., 30 minutes per day) to form relationships with one another, plan for college, discuss college applications, complete their six-year plans (a four-year high school plan, plus two of post secondary education), etc.

Improvements from the blueprint program are beginning to show in the data, said Pekel. "For the third year in a row, we're seeing our high schools hang onto a significantly higher share of the students they start with at the beginning of the year. And in any urban district, that is one of the key things you want to see as an indicator that will ultimately lead to higher graduation rates and, beyond that, college attendance."

Another indicator may come from Saint Paul Public School's involvement as one of 30 districts nationwide participating in a pilot program, titled "Successful Outcomes," with the National Association of Higher Education Registrars. Pekel said he is excited about this opportunity because it will help the district get a true measure of college attendance and not just the percentage of graduating seniors who say they are enrolling in college. Instead, this program will provide the district data on every Saint Paul Public Schools graduate who enrolls in almost any higher education institution in the country, including whether that student remains in college and, for one-third of the students, the major. Whereas the district has the measurement in place to assess its investment in graduation rate increases, which have shown significant gains across all groups, this pilot program will provide data the district currently lacks to measure its college matriculation investment, which is an even more important measure according to Pekel. He said that schools are not preparing students for graduation; they are preparing them for college and employment.

Leadership

Knuth often tells principals, "Leadership drives the organization." This belief is shared in Saint Paul Public Schools. The district's Office of Leadership Development established an intensive, three-phased leadership development program to prepare aspiring principals for leadership in Saint Paul Public Schools.

"I'm going to challenge the old myth that we have, or are presently going through, a shortage of candidates for the principalship," said St. Sauver. "That is not true at all here in Saint Paul. We had many people certified, but they are not highly qualified." Thus, with Superintendent Harvey's desire to see more highly qualified urban principals, a conviction and a grant created the Leadership Institute.

Leadership Institute applicants must: want to be a principal in the Saint Paul Public Schools; be relentless about raising expectations for urban students; possess a valid Minnesota principal's license; and have leadership experience and excellent references. And that is just for the first round of screening. Each applicant's resume, references, essay, and credentials are reviewed and scored by three principals in other Minnesota districts. Saint Paul's principals and administrators then conduct one-on-one interviews. From these, the original field is narrowed. The average number of applicants in the last three years was 60; from that, 20 to 25 candidates were selected.

Once selected, candidates become "cohort fellows" part of a cohort of leaders who will have a support network of administrative colleagues. They engage in a three-week intensive training during the summer, centered on essential competencies necessary for school leadership: as a character/role model; vision creation and leadership; staff management; resourcefulness; constructive work with others; effective constituency management; and results achievement. The first week's offsite training helps candidates learn more about themselves and their leadership style through personality testing, emotional intelligence quotient testing, and school scenario role playing. The second week is dedicated to intense training on Bolman's and Deal's "four frames of leadership:" structural, human resource, political, and symbolic. Applicants spend the third week learning more about the district's systems—from departments such as strategic planning, human resources, and budgeting—and how they impact principals' decisions.

After those three weeks, the Office of Leadership Development follows up with the candidates throughout the year and coordinates mentoring, coaching, and additional training in monthly half-day sessions. Some move into assistant principal or principal positions during the year; others remain as teachers or interns. The central office continues to help and support them for a couple of years, St. Sauver said, to build a succession planning group. None is guaranteed a principal position; instead, this group becomes the candidate pool submitted to site councils when principal vacancies arise.

Comprehensive Vision

As with every change, Saint Paul Public Schools' transformation has not been without growing pains. But, said Pekel, "In hindsight, it has worked pretty well." He and Knuth agreed that this transformation is, and continues to be, an evolutionary process. Knuth likened it to having a camera lens on a big picture framework of processes, with the most important objects increasingly coming into clear focus. Through Harvey's leadership, the action plan, and the hard work of all staff within the central office, schools, and communities, the district is at a point where the priorities are much clearer.

And, said Knuth, "In another two to three years we'll look differently than we do now, because I'm hopeful that that big picture lens on which we hang—all the quality criteria such as leadership development, process management, data-driven decision making, and continuous improvement—will be much clearer for every school in the district."

The district could not have dictated the focus from the beginning, said Knuth, because sites needed to fill in some of the details as they implemented the work. "That's important because it is site-based. Had we imposed from the beginning and then filtered it down, I don't think we would be where we are today."

Leadership determination and commitment have played a significant role in the district's progress. Pekel said this type of achievement takes time. "If you don't have the kind of time it takes to make these sorts of changes by winning hearts and minds and convincing people with data, you are really not going to have the chance to get to this hopeful point where we are." With Harvey's five-year tenure at Saint Paul—a tenure twice as long as the average urban superintendent—she has demonstrated commitment and shown results. By implementing her vision while also being responsive to schools' needs, she had led the district "a remarkable distance," said Knuth. "I've been in this district a long time. I never would have believed prior to her leadership that we could do as much as we have in as short a period of time."

The Saint Paul "school of choice" indicator that sparked the strategic plan is showing positive signs as well. "In an era of declining enrollment [for the city of Saint Paul and throughout Minnesota], the district's enrollment is not declining as quickly as other area districts," said Knuth. With the number of choices in selecting and attending area schools, she said the reality has become "a world of opportunity."

At the beginning of each school year, Harvey shares a theme that fits within the district's broader "world of opportunity" theme and encapsulates the upcoming year's challenge. Together these themes paint additional, carefully composed details on the emerging masterpiece that represents Saint Paul Public Schools' metamorphosis:

- 1999 to 2000: Raising Expectations
- 2000 to 2001: Leadership for Change
- 2001 to 2002: Focus on Student Work
- 2002 to 2003: Challenging Every Child
- 2003 to 2004: Knowing with Precision

"One of the things that has really changed since Pat Harvey came to town with all this reform has been a comprehensiveness," said St. Sauver. Prior to Harvey's tenure, only pieces of the action plan, best practices training, site-based strategic planning and empowerment, and data-based decision making existed in isolation with "no cohesiveness and no comprehension." But, St. Sauver said, "Coming together, these things have made a really strong program here at Saint Paul in the last four years."

Chapter 5

Transferring a Continuous Improvement Model Between Districts through Leadership

By Emma Skogstad

A significant factor in continuous improvement efforts is the support of senior administrators within a school district. And the presence of new administrators can provide both new ideas and uncertainty. A district in Roswell, N.M., leveraged the arrival of a new superintendent to institute an accountability program and initiate real change.

From Rio Rancho to Roswell

In 2000 there was no accountability program in place in New Mexico. Rio Rancho Public Schools, a relatively young school district, was developing a positive reputation built on student success and programs and initiatives to improve student learning. However, despite being a good school district, there was a gap in learning in subpopulations. To address this gap, the school began to disaggregate data in 2000, two years before the NCLB act made this mandatory.

Manuel (Manny) Rodriguez was hired in December 1999 as associate superintendent for curriculum and instruction, with a focus on student achievement. He reported to Rio Rancho in January 2000 and actually started the instructional process in August 2000 after professional development with principals during the 2000 spring semester. "You can imagine what we went through in implementing the disaggregation of data and action plans to address the subpopulations," said Rodriguez, whose focus was based on his experience as principal in Pasadena Texas and the process he learned from then Brazosport administrators Gerald Anderson and Pat Davenport.

Sue Cleveland, Rio Rancho superintendent, had the vision and supported all Rodriguez's efforts in the implementation of this process. Cleveland was familiar with school accountability practices from her time as a teacher and building and district administrator for technology, staff development, and federal programs in Deer Park Independent School District, near Houston. But some Rio Rancho educators were not familiar with or eager to adopt accountability practices

However, the results of the accountability program soon spoke for themselves. In the first year the program was implemented district wide, there were significant improvements in performance of subgroups. A most noteworthy example was the Puesta del Sol Elementary; in one year, the school went from having the lowest achievers to the highest achievers in the district. These results at Puesta del Sol (figures 11 and 12) caused a lot of district principals to buy into the program. And disaggregating data gave the Rio Rancho school administrators and teachers information about which students needed further assistance.

Rio Rancho followed the Brazosport model of disaggregating data by identifying areas of weakness and deficit, addressing these weaknesses in a timeline focusing consistently on areas of deficit, and assessing frequently. Teachers assessed students once per week. Unfortunately, despite the success of doing this, "This process was wrought with issues," said Rodriguez. Because the school district did not have Web-based mechanism for testing, teachers were constructing the weekly assessment themselves, a time-consuming effort.

When Rodriguez transferred to Roswell Independent School District in July 2002, he implemented the Brazosport model there as well but made adaptations based on his experiences in Rio Rancho and as a high school principal in Pasadena.

Puesta del Sol
Reading Score Changes

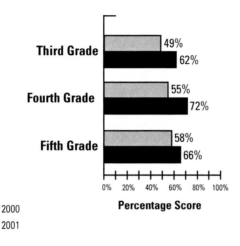

Figure 11

Puesta del Sol
Math Score Changes

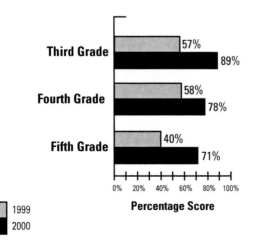

Figure 12

About Roswell

The Roswell Independent School District is the sixth largest in the State of New Mexico. Of Roswell's 9,352 students, 33 percent live at the poverty level and 62 percent are eligible for free or reduced lunches. (In some schools, as many as 99 percent are eligible for free or reduced lunches). Twenty-two percent of the adult population in Roswell is functionally illiterate, and there is an 8.3 percent unemployment rate in this rural county.

Overcoming Challenges

When Rodriguez assumed the superintendent position in July 2002, there were three principal position vacancies, a vacancy in the role of assistant superintendent for finance, and a vacancy in the role of assistant superintendent for special services. (Most administrators had been in Roswell for a period of time.) At the first meeting with principals, Rodriguez informed them that the State Department of Education, now the Public Education Department, had placed the Roswell ISD at "focused monitoring" status because of the inordinate number of students in special education. (Actually, the district received this notification in March 2002, but administrators and the school board had not been notified.)

"In addition to these opportunities, we managed to pass a $15,000,000 'go bond' that no one expected would be passed by our community," said Rodriguez. "The passing of this 'go bond' was the impetus for addressing health, safety, and compliance issues in a district and community that has not had a new facility built since the late 1960s."

One of the main challenges the district faced, in addition to the accountability practices, was simply the fact that any kind of change can be challenging. Mike Gottlieb, associate superintendent for instruction at Roswell, said: "Change is hard. Sometimes you can't wait for everybody to buy in. In a district this size, you work with administrative staff and teachers, and those people must come aboard because the lives of children are in the balance. Most (99 percent) are coming aboard. They're seeing the results of the initiatives, seeing what's working and why we're making those changes."

The Roswell school board, superintendent, and other administrators have worked to manage this transition, while focusing on moving forward for the benefit of students. Rodriguez said that students adapt much quicker and easier than most adults, although he said that many parents and community members have been supportive of the district's changes. "In any situation, there is going to be people in the system who are uncomfortable with the changes," he said. "But one focuses on students and improving the opportunities for them to improve. There's only so much time, and we focus on the things that will provide opportunities for improving student learning and student achievement."

Mary Ann Zipprich, assistant superintendent for special services, said that data disaggregation can actually be used to help convince teachers of the usefulness of the accountability. "If you use numbers [and] data, it's not subject, and it's helpful in achieving teacher buy-in," she said. And as teachers start to address the points of students' weaknesses, their data starts to improve. "This success helps people get on board," said Zipprich.

Another factor in overcoming challenges associated with accountability at Roswell has been leadership. "We have good leadership here," said Zipprich. "Certain principals stand out. They brought the others on board by saying the bar has been lifted for everyone and saying this is something we're going to live with."

Frequent Testing Improves Instruction

Roswell uses a Web-based mechanism to test students in grades 3 through 10 on an instructional focus area (i.e., a standard) once every three weeks. Unlike teachers at Rio Rancho, Roswell's teachers do not have to make their own tests every three weeks. Instead, the district purchases tests from Lightspan (which was recently purchased by PLATO Learning, an educational software company that provides tests). Lightspan sent a consultant to work with teachers to construct assessments. They created a database of questions covering simple to complex skills. The assessment covers five questions per skill, and three skills are tested every three weeks. The multiple-choice tests take students approximately 30 minutes to complete.

After students take the tests, the district receives reports showing how students performed. This data is also broken up by grades (Figure 13) and individual classrooms so students can see which questions they missed, how the class did as a total aggregate, and how subpopulations, including special education and English language learners, performed on the tests

Based on their test results, students are grouped into one of four categories:

1. enrichment (students score between 90 percent and 100 percent),
2. maintenance (students score between 80 percent and 89 percent),
3. tutorial (students score between 51 percent and 79 percent), or
4. reteaching (students score between 0 percent and 50 percent).

Students who score in the enrichment category are provided with more sophisticated levels of instruction. Reteaching and tutorial students are given instruction to address their deficit areas by grade level and content, from simple constructions to complex sequence of skills students need to pass an objective.

When the program was first implemented at Roswell, assessment was given every week; but unfortunately the school district did not have the infrastructures, specifically the bandwidth, in place for this kind of frequent testing, so the necessary adjustments were made.

In addition to the Lightspan tests, students in Roswell take the following assessments:

- two benchmark assessments, one in December and one in February;
- STAR Reading® and STAR Math® from Renaissance Learning™;
- Dynamic Indicators of Basic Early Literacy Skills (DIBELS) in kindergarten and potentially soon in first and second grade;
- the California Achievement Test;
- the state's criterion-reference tests in grades 4 and 8; and
- Brigance Assessment for Special Education, which is an inventory of skills.

Seventh Grade Testing Results

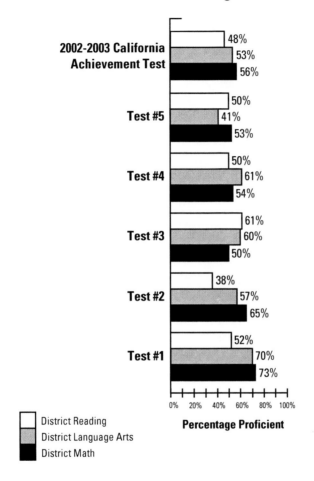

District Reading
District Language Arts
District Math

Percentage Proficient

Figure 13

"The various assessments help the district teach," said Zipprich. "In the past, assessment was typically used as pre- and post-assessment." Now, many assessments are used at Roswell on a continuous basis to help drive instruction. The results can be analyzed to determine how successful instruction has been. If students are showing that they are not picking up on what was taught, then the instruction is examined and adjusted if necessary. The district looks at how the instruction should be presented for success.

Instructional Intervention Time

Instructional intervention time, which the district has every day, is used to address student deficits ascertained by disaggregating the most recent data from the state-mandated test. Instruction is then provided in the skills, from simple to complex, of the objectives in the core content areas. The assessment—given in short, periodic intervals from one to three weeks—is the basis for determining whether the students are achieving proficiency in these skills. These skills are integrated into the core content areas, including reading, math, and language arts. According to Rodriguez, students are profiled, based on the continuous assessment results, in the instructional interventions: enrichment, maintenance, tutorial, or reteaching. Students are fluid within these groups because they are tested every three weeks, so they can move, for example, from reteaching to enrichment within a matter of weeks.

The scope and sequence for instruction is based on simple to complex skills. Rodriguez said that demonstrating proficiency in these skills allows students to make their most deficit area at the objective level a strength. Students are then able to transfer and apply skills from content across other content areas, which results in improved learning and student achievement.

Gottlieb said that by teaching through students' greatest deficit, all their skills improve. "Everything we do is a balance," he said.

Zipprich gave the example of students' test scores showing that they have a hard time identifying the main idea of a passage. Students will then receive three weeks of instructional intervention time learning about main idea, but in addition, they will also learn to be more careful readers and to think as they read along. Hence, by working on main idea, students increase their reading vocabulary and learn more about plot and characters.

Students spend 30 minutes per day studying the skills before taking the Web-based tests. Each grade level is grouped according to the assessment categories. For example, all grade 4 students at the reteaching level would be grouped together and provided with activities to address the skills in which they need more help. Zipprich stressed, however, that they do not hold students back. "When we know students have mastered things, we extend information."

Intervention for the Lower Quartile

One intervention that Rodriguez has implemented to address subpopulations in the lower quartile at Roswell involves an instructional intervention down to the student level in math, reading, and language arts skills. In language arts and reading, for example, graphic organizers are important tools for students to organize information. Students are taught the elements in story webs (i.e., title, setting, problem, action, and outcome for fiction and main idea webs for nonfiction). They apply these skills to reading and then are asked to transfer the learning to writing.

In the first week, there is an emphasis on preliminary writing, where the teacher works with students in the lower quartile to use the graphic organizers to construct preliminary writing organizational exercises. It may take the student a week to put together a story profile web. In the second week, writing, students draft a composition based on the story web by constructing paragraphs with main ideas, supporting details, and pertinent story points. These compositions are then scored based on a 6 + 1 rubric. The desired result for students using this approach is 3.5 on ideas and organization to be considered proficient. Students and teachers sit down together to revise the compositions, and by the end of the second week, students submit a finished document.

According to Rodriquez, it took a semester for this instructional intervention and progress monitoring form to be implemented in the schools, but it is now being used successfully. And appropriate modifications will be made in the continuous improvement effort to maximize instruction and student learning. Similar interventions are being used for mathematics, and teachers have begun to notice that students in the second quartile and above are also benefiting from this type of intervention.

Rodriquez noted that the district had impressive results at the end of the first year of implementation at Roswell. The 15 elementary schools exceeded typical growth in reading/language arts and mathematics by 150 percent; in all five contents, they increased growth by 141 percent. However, there is no specific focus on science and social studies because there are no grade-level specific standards for these subjects in New Mexico. Science will be added in the 2004 to 2005 school year to the instructional process, and the content will be part of state's accountability program.

Zipprich said, "Knowing student deficit areas, teaching to that, continuous assessment, a strong literacy framework, principals going into classroom more often to observe teachers working with students, instructional interventions, and progress monitoring of students in the lower quartile, all of these things combined have helped us meet the needs of all our students and our special education population."

Helping Special Education Students

Another area of significant improvement in Roswell was in special education. The school district had been under critical, focused monitoring from the state when Rodriguez assumed his position as superintendent. Out of the 9,788 students in the district, 1,339 were identified as specific learning disabled (SLD), which reflects 13.7 percent of the total population. That percentage is above the state and national averages and high above the numbers statistically expected to qualify a student as SLD. One reason for the extremely high number of students in special education programs was that the district had not been providing adequate core programs in reading, writing, and mathematics to meet the instructional needs of a diverse population of students. In the first year of implementing accountability practices and intervention practices in Roswell to address student deficits in math, reading, and language arts, results for many subgroups doubled. During the 2003 to 2004 school year, 863 students were placed back into regular education classes for 80 percent or more of the school day (up from only 528 in the 2001 to 2002 school year) through inclusionary practices. Many of them are significantly farther along now than they were at the end of the last school year because they are meeting higher expectations.

The Importance of Communication

Rodriguez said that an important part of school districts' successes is their willingness to receive and share information. "It's important to share information," said Rodriguez. The accountability methods "were learned in past experiences in Texas and adapted. All of us are a product of our experiences. The more we experience the better person we become."

Communication and collaboration have been key in successfully implementing accountability practices. "Years ago, as I began teaching, I used to feel isolated because teaching was not about dealing with other adults," said Zipprich. "You had your classroom and your students all day, and you could arrive and work with those students all day and then go home. Now, education is being transformed. Communication and collaboration in this day and age are the hallmark of education, and it's certainly been transformed in this district."

Gottlieb noted the increased communication. "The assistant superintendents are a team, and we don't get our feelings hurt anymore. ... It's a team effort. None of us wear our feelings on our sleeve. We're open to help from others."

Monitoring Schools and Staff Development

In his commitment to encouraging open communication, Rodriquez believes in being a participant in the process and so he, Gottlieb, and Zipprich made formal visits to the district's 22 schools 91 times in 2003. Questions asked during monitoring visits vary and can include items such as: How are you integrating the skills of the subjective into your core content? Are principals making observations? Which are the "lower quartile students?" And what interventions are you using with then?

Gottlieb said, "We all have deficits, and if we can support each others deficits, we'll have a stronger team."

Rodriguez and Gottlieb both stressed the importance of close monitoring of schools by administrators. According to Gottlieb, "Within the system Dr. Rodriguez has brought to Roswell, we monitor/support the administrators and teaching staff at all schools. We support what they're doing and monitor student progress. Then we determine how we can get over stumbling blocks, using professional development, sharing ideas, [and] brainstorming."

Making these visits helps address problem areas by improving communication. For example, when the accountability program first started at Roswell, teachers and principals in some schools did not believe students were doing as poorly as the data indicated. However, once administrators explained all the data, including the inclusion of lower quartile and subpopulations data, the principal and teachers were better able to understand what needed to happen next.

Gottlieb gave an example of how this understanding led to improvements in teaching: "I had a sixth grade teacher say to me 'I've known you for 23 years now. I see now that people know who these kids are in their classrooms and are making an effort to make a change.' Now that's powerful. And this teacher was against [accountability] at first. I've seen him several times. And he's saying teachers are making extra efforts to ensure kids aren't in the bottom quartile again."

Roswell school district has been recognized for its mentoring program for new teachers. Gottlieb's department developed the program for new teachers to receive faculty development and support. The district has received grants every year of $35,000 to $45,000 per year based on this mentoring program.

First, teachers receive a week of paid in-service, along with $35,000 worth of material. Teachers are given additional instruction on a four-block method including guided reading instruction, self-selected reading instruction, writing, and vocabulary. Teachers are shown how to use this method with special education and bilingual students. They are also given instruction in teaching math, monitoring students for safety factors, and using and interpreting data.

After the week of in-service, new teachers are assigned to a building and a grade-level mentor. A district committee meets with new teachers four times a year to help them with concerns and needs. Another full-time person is dedicated to helping new teachers whenever they need it. "We ask, 'What can we do to help them?' and 'Where are they having problems?'" said Gottlieb. "If education's not the right choice, it's about helping them find where they should be. It's not about 'I got you—I'm going to tell the administrators.' I don't allow that." Instead, support is provided over a three-year period to help teachers succeed.

One important aspect of professional development is finding the right people to help teachers learn. For example, Roswell has hired bilingual experts to teach how to succeed in dual-language schools. In an effort to support teachers' efforts to improve data, the district also offers workshops that are voluntarily attended by teachers. Teachers are given incentives to attend these them, including a stipend, good presenters, and $30 to $100 worth of topic-specific supplies so when they go into the classroom, they have what they need to implement what they have learned.

Through monitoring and staff development programs, teachers are receiving significant support on different ways to work with data. The district believes it is critical to have a professional development program that aligns with district goals and is sufficiently funded.

The district now has quickly gained tangible results in student achievement, with the help of supportive administrators and the lessons learned by other districts. This district exemplifies the key principle that strong leaders and an openness to external ideas are critical in continuous improvement.

Chapter 6

Florida District Learns from Challenges in Implementing the Eight-step Process

By Lee Simons

Anne Lindsay knew she was on to something when she first heard Gerald Anderson speak. Anderson, a former superintendent of the Brazosport Independent School District, was extolling to Florida educators the benefits of using continuous improvement methods typically used in the corporate world.

Lindsay, the director of curriculum and instruction at Highlands County Schools, said it was something close to an epiphany. "When I heard his data about Brazosport, I was just going, 'Oh, my gosh. This sounds just like Highlands County.' The demographics were identical. The performance of our students was identical, and the total student populations were similar."

Their challenges were also the same. How does a school district close the achievement gap between its highest-performing students in wealthier schools and minority students who attend poorer schools? That question had plagued Lindsay and her colleagues for years.

Located in the heart of Florida, Highlands County is primarily an agricultural region, home to citrus, beef, and dairy producers. It has also become home for thousands of migrant workers, many of whom stay year-round thanks to the region's ability to grow through all four seasons.

Highlands County Schools has seen a steady rise in the number of Hispanic and African American students over the past several years. Of the district's 11,730 students, 70 percent are white, 15 percent are African American, 14 percent are Hispanic, and one percent is Asian.

Whereas many migrant families must shuttle to different parts of the country to find work, those in Highlands County are less mobile and more willing to stay put. That places pressure on educators to find ways of ensuring the district's poorer students have access to the same opportunities for achievement as students hailing from wealthier schools. The challenge is not lost on Lindsay, who believes the Brazosport story was the impetus her fellow administrators needed to begin making significant changes within Highlands' 15 schools.

"I loved his story," she said of Anderson's presentation. "His methodology was so systematic. It's what you do every day. It's just natural, logical steps and processes that teachers really do already, if they're doing what they need to be doing. We realized maybe we weren't doing that."

Back to the Drawing Board

After hearing Anderson's presentation in 2000, Lindsay returned to Highlands County with a new mindset for pursuing continuous improvement in her district. At the time a middle-school principal, she and other principals had been encouraged to begin making more of their instructional decisions based on data such as assessment scores to help improve curriculum and instruction.

So Lindsay shared Anderson's data with her superintendent at the time, who was also familiar with his work and agreed that the Brazosport approach could indeed work in Highlands County. The need for change was immediate, and the district had to begin changing attitudes among principals, teachers, and even parents about raising the bar on educational standards.

The district invited Anderson to speak at its summer training session for administrators in 2001. Anderson addressed the eight-step process and how other schools might adopt it to work for them. The plan-do-check-act instructional cycle for K-12 education struck an immediate chord among Highlands County administrators. How they would adapt it to their own needs, said Lindsay, was not as easy to figure out.

Although she believed in the concept, Lindsay did not immediately take the ideas back to her own school. Instead, she worked with a state-funded resource center near Highlands County that served as an arm of the Tallahassee School Improvement Office. The resource center was part of a state support network dedicated to implementing strategies to enhance student achievement. "We decided we wanted, as a group, to take the concepts we had heard and see if we could use them as a foundation for a grassroots effort to improve the way we manage our school system on the curriculum side to bring about greater student achievement," she said.

With the help of resource center staff members, Lindsay—who was now director of curriculum and instruction—and her colleagues examined the eight-step process through the lens of Highlands County's educational priorities. They asked themselves what the process should look like according to their own needs and state guidelines.

Lindsay took her ideas and plugged them into a possible training program for teachers. She worked closely with Jo Anna Cochlin, presently a coordinator of secondary and vocational work with the district; and Pat Lee, who is now a curriculum/literacy resource teacher at Lake Placid High School.

Together, Lindsay, Cochlin and Lee massaged what they believed planning might look like in Florida schools. They agreed that the steps in the planning phase should include curriculum alignment and mapping, textbook review, data analysis, and an instructional calendar.

The district provides a template to teachers to develop curriculum maps of their own. (It is based on curriculum mapping expert Heidi Hayes-Jacobs' process for curriculum mapping, but has its own distinct Highlands County angle.) Then the district got teachers to investigate the content of the textbooks to ensure that it matched their maps. Gaps are typically found in the textbook material, said Lindsay, so teachers are aware that they have to look beyond the text to find the content that students need.

Emily Bauer is one of the teachers who helped push the process early on. A seventh-grade and curriculum resources teacher at Sebring Middle School, Bauer is in charge of facilitating workshops to help teachers get the resources they need to use the right curriculum. "We had the curriculum resource teachers from many schools get together and learn about the process and see results as they were implemented by Brazosport," Bauer said. "We were really gung-ho about it."

The Florida Comprehensive Assessment Test (FCAT) provides the district's most consistent data to teachers for grades 3 through 10 in reading and math. Scores are reported by grade level for the district, school, and teacher. The district is developing a data analysis method because most teachers are never taught how to analyze data from both quantitative or qualitative standpoints. That data is then used to develop an instructional focused calendar.

"The instructional focused calendar is the big picture of content that must be taught throughout the school year," Lindsay said. "We like to refer to this as the macro-lesson planning process. Based on the data, this is where the focus needs to be over the calendar year to be sure the content that the students are weakest in gets covered prior to FCAT in March of each year."

The macro-lesson planning process is closely followed by a micro plan, which results in content pacing guides that teachers can then use for their students. Further micro plans finally develop into what become the daily lesson plans that teachers can use for a week or several weeks at a time.

The planning phase was conducted with one eye firmly fixed on standards. "The very first thing we had to do was identify that our instruction had to be grounded in Florida Sunshine State Standards and ensure our teachers knew what those were," Lindsay said.

Florida's Sunshine State Standards were approved by the State Board of Education in 1996 to provide expectations for student achievement. They were written in seven subject areas, each divided into four separate grade clusters (pre-K–2, 3-5, 6-8, and 9-12). Lindsay stated that the district simply cannot be assured that all teachers are fully committed to teaching content of the Sunshine State Standards.

Although the standards had been in place for 10 years, Lindsay was not confident that Highlands County teachers understood that they should be driving instructional content. How would teachers be brought up to speed quickly and successfully? "We have been using the terms such as 'curriculum mapping' and assuming that everyone understands," Lindsay said. "We realize now that the assumptions were wrong. We are in a 'start over' phase this year."

That includes the development of curriculum leadership teams at each school that work with the principal to "redo" the Highlands County version of the plan-do-check-act instructional cycle. It also involves providing more training to teachers and principals throughout the planning process.

"We found that the principal cannot be the lone ranger in the instructional leadership roles, and he/she needs key people throughout the school who get the PDCA process and what it looks like when it is implemented," Lindsay said.

Crafting the Plan and Acting on It

First and foremost, Lindsay said they needed a clear picture of what their curriculum should be. Answering that question was more than simple data disaggregation and calendar development, she said. The most significant challenge the district continues to face is reaching agreement as a body of teachers and educators on the essential content of the curriculum, as well as overcoming discrepancies within grade levels in how the content is presented.

So Lindsay and her team asked teachers to draw a macro plan of the curriculum they needed to cover for the year. At that point, planners—including the district's curriculum staff, staff from the Suncoast Area Center for Educational Enhancement, principals, assistant principals, and two lead teachers from each site—infused a curriculum mapping method based on Hayes-Jacobs' work into teachers' plans. "We said that they need to articulate with other teachers and across, below, and above you what your curriculum will be so that it is aligned with the Sunshine State Standards," Lindsay said.

Such momentous curriculum changes met with initial skepticism among teachers, who viewed the changes as more work heaped on top of their regular teaching responsibilities. Lindsay said the district still has to work to overcome misconceptions about the process, the main one being that the plan-do-check-act cycle steers teachers away from actually teaching their students.

After articulating the need to share curriculum plans, Lindsay said it was time to go ahead and teach it. "Once you're clear about curriculum content pieces, do it," she said.

Acting on the plan raised a number of questions for district administrators. What is direct instruction? What is a mini-lesson? How do I teach a mini-lesson and integrate it into the existing curriculum?

Highlands County teachers had already indicated their desire for an instructional focus calendar and mini-lessons to provide maintenance on certain subjects to students who needed it the most throughout the year. Introduced in the Brazosport project, mini-lessons are 10- to 15-minute lessons addressing specific state standards that are taught four days a week, typically followed by an assessment conducted on Friday. Based on how students perform on those assessments, teachers then decide whether individual students need remediation, enrichment, or an outright reteach of the material.

Lindsay and her team realized the best way to begin answering these questions was to get teachers to look at student assessment data. "Once we worked on curriculum mapping, the next piece was looking at the data," she said. "The only data we had was FCAT. When they report the FCAT back to us, we get a writing score, and a FCAT Sunshine State score in reading and math."

Reading scores are broken into four clusters that indicate how many points a student scored in each cluster. They also show each school average for reading, as well as the district average. However, they do not indicate what specific objectives were mastered or not mastered by a student. Math scores are similarly reported in five strands. The test reports how many points a student earned out of a possible total for each strand. For the writing portion, a score of 0 to 6 is given.

"When we look at that data, you could interpret the data to tell you what areas in reading or math students were performing better or worse in," Lindsay said. "We use them to determine weak to strong areas."

Administrators began analyzing the test data from weak to strong performance and then reordered critical content based on what students needed the most help in. For Highlands County Schools, this represented the crux of the "do" part of the process, Lindsay said. "We had to spend time learning about how you do the 'do' correctly," she said.

Enter mini-lessons. The district began pulling teachers to write mini-lessons that broke down standard benchmarks into critical components. Whereas the state's standards are very broad, she said, teachers had to know what critical content a child must demonstrate proficiency in.

"We were spending the time to break that down and then developed modeled, scripted mini-lessons to make sure they're modeling for the students how to utilize skills that they need to be a better problem solver and critical thinker," Lindsay said. "It was a challenge for us. Our teachers said, 'Find somebody who's already written these lessons.' They didn't have time to develop them."

Highlands County Schools did not have the resources to allow teachers the time to write mini-lessons. After investing a great deal of time and money on the idea, Lindsay said the district is not where it needs to be in terms of making them a regular part of the curriculum. "We are still hanging on the use of a mini-lesson to target specific skills on the Sunshine State Standards," she said. "We worked on the model and what it looks like. As a district-wide, consortium-wide understanding, we're nowhere near that."

Presently, Highlands County teachers are following their own individual instructional calendars as they see fit. With a special emphasis placed on a Literacy First campaign in 2003, teachers were hard pressed to spend more time on adhering to the plan-do-check-act, but at least a better understanding of the process now exists, Bauer said. "It has helped me to throw out things that keep me busy that don't have a basis for spending time on," Bauer said.

Check-up and Act

Administrators at Highlands County Schools decided it was time to move on to the "check" part of the eight-step model, even though the initial phases were not necessarily fully implemented. It was crucial, said Lindsay, that teachers process-monitor their students to determine whether they had developed skills necessary in demonstrating proficiency.

"We were very sketchy in all phases. We assumed a lot about knowledge and understanding of the process in general and what it looks like when you do each phase," Lindsay said. "We tried to do it all, and it was too overwhelming for most of us. That's why we are revisiting each step and clearly defining what it looks like when you do each step. … We are only focusing this year on clarifying and training in the plan parts."

Until now, the concept of monitoring students through mini-assessments administered regularly has been nil in Florida, according to Lindsay. This challenged district administrators to develop a check process. "We needed to get more into line of short, quick progress monitoring assessments," she said.

Getting teachers to act on those assessments proved to be an even bigger problem. "This threw them over the edge," Lindsay said. "What we were trying to say is that even though your kids don't get it, you need to do something for them. In the 'act' process, what we were saying is after you assess, you have to decide whether they need remediation, enrichment, or do you move on? We had all kinds of questions and concerns on that end."

Lindsay's team worked to develop a bank of mini-assessments that were correlated to the essential content of the Sunshine State Standards benchmarks. It proved overwhelming, as they tried to identify knowledgeable teachers to help develop the assessments. It was too much to ask teachers to leave their students and spend days developing this bank of assessments.

The implementation process turned the district upside down, Lindsay said. Teachers were suddenly getting more direction from district staff than they ever had before, in addition to being asked to do more than what they were already doing in the classroom. The inability to counter the "something else I have to do" mentality has proven a huge barrier, Lindsay said. "It is happening, but we have not spent enough time with our schools to make sure we're moving forward," she said.

Bauer said a lack of consistent curriculum has stopped all teachers from enthusiastically getting on board the process. "Teachers had traditionally been left up to their own to deliver the benchmarks.

To hold teachers accountable, we needed curriculum and assessments that were the same," Bauer said.

Bauer is nonetheless an advocate of the plan-do-check-act instructional cycle. Every teacher at Sebring has a bank of mini-lessons and assessments to use, albeit a very small bank (mini-lessons and assessments presently last a teacher about a fourth of the school year). And the process has helped teachers rely on each others' resources more than ever before.

"What I really like is that now my mindset is changed in a way that I don't just look for lessons that I want to teach," Bauer said. "I really focus now on what it is I want them to be able to do. That has permeated everything I do."

The district decided in 2002 to develop a comprehensive training program that infused the Sunshine State Standards, bringing in every principal, assistant principal, and two lead teachers from each school for a three-day session on the plan-do-check-act cycle. The intent was to train these individuals and have them return to their respective schools and pass along their knowledge.

The district reserved a series of days to train teachers and then had them start revising their curriculum maps and instructional calendars to reflect an emphasized assessment plan. But the plan fell apart when the district simply could not produce enough mini-lessons to meet students' instructional needs. "The assessments needed to be correlated to the mini-lessons to determine if they were on track. We just saw it as an additional layer of testing that we needed to provide other than what the teacher gave on a normal basis," Lindsay said. "They perceived mini-lessons in addition to what they were going to teach each day. We struggled with that concept, and last year it basically stopped."

Momentarily, the plan-do-check-act approach had come to a standstill in Highlands County. The district's lack of resources far outweighed teachers' ability to properly assess students in line with state standards and with the eight-step process.

A New Hope

The 2003 to 2004 school year just might paint a brighter picture for the process in Highlands County. Turnover in the district level has paved the way for a better shot at implementation. "Now we're in our third year, and we're clear about what we have to do: develop strong instructional leaders beyond principals to help the principals lead the plan-do-check-act process," Lindsay said. "We've got to have lead teachers who get it, train it, support it, know it, breathe it, do it, and mentor other teachers. We're now in the process of identifying those lead teachers. We're going to train them in their leadership role and what their expectations are."

The district's first priority will be to address the process at its three high schools, which have all received "C" grades from the state based on assessment scores. Lindsay hopes that leadership teams from each school will be fully trained by the end of the 2003 to 2004 school year. Each team will consist of three members from each school who serve as curriculum leaders. Those teams will continue to work through the summer months in training other teachers and administrators.

"I believe our schools had lost their focus on what we were here for," Lindsay said. "Our high schools had not embraced the understanding that our students are held accountable to proficiency in Sunshine State Standards."

Despite putting on the brakes after the last school year, Lindsay said the process did meet some success (Figure 14). In 2001 Highlands County had only four "A-B" schools out of 15; the rest were graded "C" and "D." The following year saw seven "A-B"

Continuous Improvement in Highlands

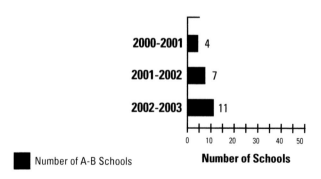

Figure 14

schools, and in 2003 there were 11 such schools in the district—a direct result of work on continuous improvement.

"I think the major achievement was that teachers were thinking more about aligning the taught curriculum with the tested curriculum," said Lindsay. "We still have individuals say, 'We are teaching to the test.' We counter that with, 'The content of the curriculum should be the benchmarks of the Sunshine State Standards.' If you teach this content and the FCAT is testing what is taught, then we are aligning well the taught and tested curriculum."

And despite initial roadblocks to implementation, Lindsay nonetheless credits much of the districts' hard-won continuous improvement successes to diving into the plan-do-check-act instructional cycle. "It gave us focus, meaning, and direction. It guided our thoughts in a systematic way," Lindsay said. "Everything may not have been perfect, but overall our principals embraced the concept, saw its relevance, and said, 'We're with you.'"

In the Highlands County school district as a whole, some closing of the achievement gap among subgroups of students can be seen, but not significantly enough to declare a complete success, Lindsay said. Some changes for the better have occurred, however; and convincing more teachers that it is due to the process will be key in continuing the improvement.

Coincidentally, help has recently come in the form of the state's recent introduction of an assessment plan that closely mirrors the eight-step process. It calls on teachers to diagnose skill deficiencies among students and monitor their progress to ensure they stay on track toward meeting standards. "It's just a good systematic process for raising student achievement," Lindsay said. "That has helped us greatly, because it aligns with plan-do-check-act."

Perhaps the biggest lesson learned in Highlands County is that the plan-do-check-act cycle is more a slow burn than an immediate process. The district needed to be clear about each step in each phase, how teachers would be taught, and teach it in "chunks" rather than all at once, she added.

"You must understand the learning styles of the school-based staff," Lindsay said. "I have found in my experience very few want to see the big picture. Most just want to know it in steps or pieces.

Then, over time, they begin to see how each piece fits into the overall picture."

While the state has asked districts to begin implementing the process for K-3, Highlands County has already begun implementation in all grades. "We didn't wait," said Lindsay. "We bit the bullet and said, 'We're going to do the same thing for all children.' It's all blended very well."

As of spring 2004, Sebring Middle School teachers were lucky to have about a fourth of the mini-lessons and assessments they needed to properly teach standards-based content to their students, Bauer said. "We don't have them written for every benchmark," she said. "All the teachers need to get it straight from the horse's mouth. They need to see the same Brazosport people. We need to see an actual school that has implemented this well and look at what to do next. If we could bypass reinventing the wheel, then we might start getting somewhere."

After realizing that the district moved too fast too soon in implementing the plan-do-check-act cycle, it has been helpful to see that state standards are quickly beginning to align with the process, Lindsay said. What worked in Brazosport can most certainly be molded into a workable concept that eventually provides teachers the tools they need to assess and work with students who need objective focus the most.

"It has truly helped us in our thinking to revamp the way from the district level that we support teachers in their professional development," Lindsay said. "It is a guide that we look to and use as we plan from the district level what we need to do to support our teachers."

Chapter 7

How a District Improved by Making the Brazosport Experience Its Own

By Peggy Newton

At 8:05 every school morning except Friday, all the fourth graders in Walt Disney Elementary School move. They leave the familiarity of their regular classrooms and divide into groups.

Some students go with a grade 4 teacher for "enrichment-plus," a long-term, project-based activity. These students play the stock market game, and once a week, a professional stockbroker comes in to advise them. Members of another group accompany aides to a classroom where they become deeply involved in the study of Native American cultures. Two teachers wait for their 11-member groups to assemble and then begin a tutorial on area, perimeter, and volume. One teacher is working with a group on a reading skill: making predictions. After 30 minutes, the students go back to their regular classrooms. The transition seems effortless because the children know where to go and what supplies they have to bring.

The orderly procession is just one outward sign of the three-year-old process that has transformed Penn-Harris-Madison schools. The initiative, called "focused instruction," meets each child at his or her point of need. Since the initiative's implementation, the district's scores have risen dramatically.

Walt Disney is one of 11 elementary schools in Penn-Harris-Madison School Corp., which serves approximately 10,000 students in northern Indiana. Its enrollment is growing, and it currently has one high school and three middle schools, in addition to the elementary schools (five of which are Title I schools).

Defining the Issue

In 2000 the school board issued an edict to the superintendent: "Find a way to improve the achievement of this district, close the gap between the achievers and non-achievers, and provide enrichment opportunities for those who show proficiency." The superintendent, Vickie Markavitch, took the order to heart and began to research what others had done to meet such challenges.

Markavitch began by establishing a set of beliefs that challenged the district's staff to have high academic expectations for all students (Figure 15). She then established goals that reflected the belief that all children could learn. The goals stated that all the district students would be reading, writing, and doing math at grade level by the end of grade 3. Another goal was that every grade 10 student could meet the standards of Indiana's graduation qualifying exam.

To reinforce and achieve widespread buy-in for these beliefs, Markavitch asked innovative educators to share their philosophies with the district. Lawrence Lezotte, founder of the Effective Schools League (a membership community of educators) spoke, as did Michael Schmoker (author of *Results: The Key to Continuous School Improvement*, Association for Supervision & Curriculum Development, 1999), and Douglas Reeves (chairman and founder of

---

The beliefs developed by a community-based strategic planning committee are visible in the schools and on the Web site. They form the basis of the district culture.

1. Instruction and learning is our priority.
2. The instructional program should establish high academic expectations for all students.
3. There should be congruence among and accountability for curriculum, instruction, and assessment.
4. The principal is the instructional leader of the school.
5. Education is a collaborative responsibility shared by students, teachers, parents, and community members.
6. A respectful, safe, and nurturing environment should be maintained.
7. The continuous professional growth of a quality staff is essential.

Figure 15

the Center for Performance Assessment, an organization dedicated to improving student achievement).

Markavitch is a long-time member of the Effective Schools League. Through the network, she met Gerald Anderson, former superintendent of Brazosport Independent School District, and heard his story of how a district in Texas improved the test scores of all students regardless of their race, gender, or socioeconomic status.

She thought Penn-Harris-Madison could make similar dramatic improvements, even though the district was not doing poorly overall. Gene Hollenberg, the principal of the district's Grissom Middle School, said, "We've always had decent test scores, but we needed a vehicle to close the achievement gap between the affluent students and those who were at risk." Would a district that was not poised on the brink of disaster have the will and energy to transform itself into a high-achieving organization?

Markavitch decided to take the Brazosport story back to Penn-Harris-Madison. She invited Anderson to conduct a two-day workshop; the first day provided an overview, and the second addressed principals and their staffs. District personnel realized that Penn-Harris-Madison shared many demographics with Brazosport; both had extreme differences among socioeconomic groups. The administrators examined the gap.

According to Principal Hollenberg, children in the district's Title I schools have a greater proportion of family-based disadvantages and lack exposure to life experiences. The children are often less verbal than those in the more affluent schools, and many have language development delays. District administrators also found that some student populations lacked basic health care.

Markavitch noticed that some schools' staff did not expect as much of the students from disadvantaged backgrounds as they expected of students from affluent backgrounds. Hollenberg said that educators believed poor students were overwhelmed by societal issues and did not hold either the students or themselves accountable for failure, but consistently asked affluent students to perform at higher levels. They needed a new approach.

As the year of research and planning came to an end, Markavitch and her staff realized they could make the Brazosport model uniquely their own. In 2001 they began to implement the focused instruction initiative, which was based on the model. Six elementary schools and one middle school decided to adopt the process.

Tammy Matz was assigned the role of focused instruction coordinator. According to Lynn Johnson, the principal of Walt Disney Elementary School, the decision to hire a coordinator was critical. "A process like this could take place in separate schools, but you would have inconsistencies," said Johnson. "Tammy is the reason that success was achieved so rapidly; she provided leadership throughout the schools."

Matz began by telling the staff that focused instruction was not an initiative that would come in for a while, visit, and leave. She explained it as a process, a way to do business in 2001 and into the future.

Like the Brazosport model, the focused instruction initiative was based on Total Quality Management (TQM) tools. W. Edwards Deming developed the tools in the 1950s so that businesses would become successful, and educators trained in TQM can use Deming's tools to ensure success in the classroom. Deming believed that improvement should be continuous and follow a cycle in which test results point workers (and teachers) to what their next steps should be. His methods require frequent assessments and then actions based on the assessments. The Brazosport model involved an eight-step process that incorporated continuous improvement. Penn-Harris-Madison decided to use the same eight steps.

Step 1: Test Score Disaggregation

The first step of the process is "test score disaggregation." The district uses the ISTEP (the Indiana Statewide Testing for Educational Progress), the same instrument that helps it determine if it is making annual yearly progress under the No Child Left Behind act. Biannually, the district administers NWEA (Northwest Evaluation Association) level tests to grades 2 through 8. The information is studied to determine student growth trends and to determine which skills are most needed for continued growth. Specifically, student subgroups are compared to provide the data necessary to progress toward closing the achievement gap.

Curriculum-embedded testing is also important and is regularly conducted through the year in reading, writing, and mathematics.

Step 2: Timeline Development

The next step is the development of instructional timelines based on the priorities that the data indicate. Each year teachers within a school determine the pace of study based on two criteria: how successful their team (grade 4 and grade 5 teachers) were at presenting the skill and how each group of students (those eligible for free and reduced priced lunches, English language learners, females, etc.) performed during the previous year on related skills. These factors may either increase or decrease the time spent on a skill.

One of the teachers' responsibilities is to put the state standards into language that parents can understand easily so that parents will be able to work with their children. Administrators create a timeline for parents, and on the school's Web site, parents can access the instructional calendar. An excerpt from Walt Disney Elementary focused instruction page follows.

Kindergarten:
Math - Addition of facts to 5; Subtraction of facts to 5
Reading - Letter recognition; Letter sounds
Grade 1:
Math - Problem solving; Reads and interprets a simple pictograph or bar graph
Reading - Contractions; Identifies sequence of events

The staff of Virgil Grissom Middle School (the only middle school involved in focused instruction) communicates the calendar to students as part of the closed-circuit announcements that are given daily. The school has a scrolling electronic message board on closed-circuit television that includes the focused skills.

Step 3: Instruction

The next step is the delivery of instruction. Although delivery is the chief responsibility of the subject teachers for each grade level, every adult in the building is involved. Grade 4 math teachers may be focusing on area, perimeter, and volume, and the physical education and music teachers may reinforce the concepts in their own lesson plans. For example, the Virgil Grissom Middle School has block scheduling with four 85-minute periods during the day. During a two-day period, students attend all eight of their classes. In the first 10 minutes of a language arts class, the teacher may explain "predicting outcomes" as a focused reading skill and have a regular curriculum for the rest of the period. The curriculum may include other opportunities to practice predicting outcomes, and the focused skill may be reinforced throughout the school by all teachers, including music, art, and physical education.

Quarterly, all middle school teachers are responsible for submitting a list of the skills they have reinforced. Practical arts, physical education, science, social studies, and music teachers document both the math and reading skills that they have reinforced during the period.

Step 4: Assessment

The district creates assessments from tests that are published by CTB McGraw Hill (a test-writing company for ISTEP). A summer workgroup comprised of teachers create or revise a mastery assessment, a tutorial assessment, and a maintenance assessment for each skill in reading and math for every level from kindergarten through grade 8. These tests are administered during the upcoming year to measure student achievement as part of Step 5 below.

For some, kindergarten may seem too early to start formal assessments, but administrators believe that beginning "from the ground up" is important. According to Principal Johnson, five-year-olds become accustomed to their biweekly assessments on specific kindergarten standards.

Steps 5 and 6: Tutorials and Enrichment

Immediately after a two-week focus period, the students take the mastery assessment on the focused skill. If a student does not achieve 80 percent on the assessment, then he or she follows a tutorial loop (generally taught by certified teachers) for two weeks. The students who master the assessments go into an enrichment loop taught by certified teachers assisted by teachers' aides and members of the community. In both the elementary and middle school, a time period is set aside for enrichment and tutorial.

For students in the grade 4 and above, enrichment is divided into two parts: regular enrichment and "enrichment-plus." Some students are permanently assigned to enrichment-plus because they achieve high scores on the district assessment. These children do long-term projects that are more challenging for them. At the beginning of the school year, administrators use reading, language, and mathematics tests published by NWEA to identify students for enrichment-plus. At the middle school, they select those who score in the top 5 percent in two of the three subjects. Most of the students are assigned to the enrichment-plus group for a year at a time. If an enrichment-plus student does not pass an assessment, then he or she must demonstrate mastery of the skill before rejoining the enrichment group. (It may take only one or two days in tutorial for the student to master the skill and go back to the enrichment-plus group.)

During any two-week time period, some members of a second group may be eligible for enrichment, and some may go into the tutorial loop. The second type of enrichment mirrors a two-week period cycle. Regular enrichment activities often involve an aspect of the focused skill, but sometimes relate to science or social studies.

For those who are in the tutorial loop, a tutorial assessment ensures that the focused skills have been mastered. If students do not pass the tutorial assessment, then they are helped until they do. Children are given opportunities throughout the year to show proficiency.

Steps 7 and 8: Maintenance and Monitoring

"Maintenance" includes a third assessment, which teachers administer approximately two weeks after the tutorial assessment. The teachers want to know if the students remember information about, for example, the perimeter of a circle or the main idea of a story. Quarterly, the middle school's math and language arts teachers document the skills that they have maintained during the time period.

Assessments have helped the district drive financial decisions. If elementary principals and staff continually see that reading skills, for example, are poor, then they may choose to spend resources on supplementing reading material. The middle school teachers, on the other hand, use more of a team approach. The teachers and the principal meet regularly to discuss data and determine how to approach the issues. The principal understands through the dialogue of the teachers what they are doing and what needs to be done in the classrooms.

For the first time, Walt Disney Elementary School displays its grade-level proficiency charts for the entire school to see. Focused instruction has led to a healthy competition, according to Johnson. When classes reach 90 percent proficiency, the students receive a star. The first grade students have a star in every reading and math skill, and other grade levels show 90 percent, with a few skills reaching at least 80 percent proficiency

Enablers of Success

Focused instruction has been successful because it has several important enablers.

The first is high-level support. Some of Penn-Harris-Madison's sister districts have tried to implement an eight-step process of their own. The coordinator believes that the difference between other schools and Penn-Harris-Madison is the support provided by the school board and superintendent. "You have to be committed to it, and that commitment has to be widespread, involving everyone," said Matz. "There are schools across the United States that are trying this on their own. I just don't know if they will see the results that we did because ours was supported from the top down."

A second enabler was adequate funding. Implementing focused instruction was expensive. The corporation paid $72,000 in consulting fees to APQC, and Johnson doubts the initiative could have succeeded without its help. The corporation also sought financial support from the school board and the federal government. Each person who is paid with Title I funds has focused instruction responsibilities. The program coordinator's salary was paid through Title I funding and was split among the schools that were participating. Title I funds currently purchase some of the needed supplies and provide some of the relief time for teachers so that they can fulfill focused instruction responsibilities. General funds from the district are targeted to the middle school participant, because the middle school receives limited funding from the Title I grant. Administrators agree that Title I does not come close to meeting all of the needs of the program.

The district itself has made a significant commitment to staff development, and focused instruction schools spend development dollars to support the process. Staff development funds pay for substitutes, release time, and process checks. In 2001 Walt Disney received Title II grant monies through St. Mary's College. Although the district no longer receives the Title II grant, St. Mary's student-teachers continue to work at Walt Disney twice a week and be trained in the focused instruction process.

The third enabler is additional time. The coordinator, superintendent, and board realized that teachers would have to be freed of their various commitments so that they could spend time with focused instruction. The district gave release time to plan lessons. Writing assessments takes time, so the coordinator brought a group together during the summer to create a year's worth of assessments, which took the burden off of the teachers, which empowered teachers to focus on instruction. (Teachers created the first year's calendar together during the staff development day prior to the school year beginning.)

To help teachers manage their time, Hollenberg presented teachers with a priority list. He highlighted the items that absolutely must be done. (For example, staff meetings are a priority.) He released them from other areas of accountability. He said, "Part of the tradeoff is that we have to move some of our extended curriculum into the enrichment period, so that students in need are able to have significant instruction in basic skills."

The fourth enabler is on-the-job training. No one could foresee how a process such as focused instruction would unfold. Matz said, "We were all learning as we were going." Principals provided ongoing staff development to support their staff in this process.

In late July 2001 she and the assistant superintendent traveled to a conference in Ontario, Calif. presented by APQC. "We spent all our time writing and learning and going to every possible thing we could," said Matz. "We knew we would have to implement it during the summer. Everything I learned at the Ontario conference I used to put the wheels in motion here when I came back."

District staff understood the process quickly because they received APQC's Total Quality Management training. The attendees from the middle school included the principal, a curriculum coordinator, two individuals from each grade level, and two other teachers (one representing the arts and one representing physical education). All of the principals brought their team leaders, at least four per building, to training.

During staff development days, APQC consultants presented the eight-step process to all of the personnel in every building. However, no one was forced to attend these meetings; those who were there wanted to be there.

The fifth enabler was coordination and consistency among schools. The process and the basic structure of focused instruction are virtually identical from school to school. The activities, which are teacher-created, may vary.

And the sixth enabler was a sharing environment. Focused instruction does not work without collaboration from the top down. Markavitch established the culture of sharing, and she is willing to share with any other district or corporation. Activities improve each year because of the sharing that occurs from building to building. Focused instruction principals meet bimonthly. During a recent meeting, the principals examined enrichment activities to achieve consistency and share what was working and what was not. One principal learned that she was the only one including grade 3 in enrichment, a practice that was stretching her resources too thin. She decided to provide enrichment to grades 4 and 5 only, so that she could target her resources on those two groups. "We provide opportunities for people to just sit down and talk about what is going on," said Hollenberg. "It is through these discussions that we continue to keep the program alive and the process evolving."

The seventh enabler is simply having a core group. In December 2003 and January 2004, Matz brought a team together conduct maintenance assessments. Engaging at least one teacher from each school and one teacher from each grade level, she selected individuals who are devoted to the process and have a deep knowledge of the curriculum. Matz uses the core group to communicate quickly and effectively with the entire school network.

The final enabler is the ability to adapt. "Any process can work if everyone buys in," said Hollenberg. "The trick is to tailor a process to our own building, needs, and demographics. They were wonderful at Brazosport to develop a process that could be adapted to everyone if they chose."

Results

In 2001 initial skeptics demanded supporting data. Within a year, the district could point to positive changes in the ISTEP rating of "percentage students proficient."

Principal Johnson said that focused instruction has raised the level of commitment of the entire staff. Teachers feel better because they know that students are getting what they need, and each year they come to the classroom better prepared from being involved in the process during previous years. She remembers that in 2001 a few educators did not want to be involved. They resisted because they had a limited amount of time and the feeling that they were already doing the best they could do. "We all found out that even though we were all trying our best, we could always do better," said Johnson. "The teachers have grown, and they know it. They feel more capable because success breeds success. Now when they look at the data, they see how far we have come. Teachers see how much difference their efforts have made to kids, and they find the feeling uplifting."

Principal Johnson notes that children are taking responsibility for their own learning and putting pressure on their teachers. The grade 1 students like the idea of receiving grade-level stars and know that the stars indicate proficiency. "There is a healthy competition in the school," said Johnson. "Kids now talk about learning. They tell me the grades they receive on their assessments. There is a whole cultural change. It began with the staff and principals, and now parents and students are involved." The principal said the attitude is positive among staff and students. And students remark that the days go by quickly.

Matz said that focused instruction has allowed the teachers to take a hold of their instructional time and use it more effectively. "They believe that every minute and every day counts. Groups taking field trips do their focused instruction on the bus going to the destination."

The district has seen several dramatic jumps in proficiency. It reviews the percentage of students recognized as proficient on the state exam. In 2001 the district's Elm Road Elementary School scored 52 percent proficient on ISTEP. In 2002 and 2003 it jumped to 64 percent proficient.

The principal of Grissom Middle School has compared data from the grade 8 students with the data he collected in 2001, when the students were in grade 6. In English language arts, only 50 percent of the students passed the state assessment in 2001. As eighth graders, 68 percent of the students passed. Even more importantly, the students who receive free and reduced-price lunches made an average jump in scores of 22 percent.

In 2001, 58 percent of the grade 6 students passed the math test. Now that these students are in grade 8, 84 percent passed. The group that receives free and reduced-price lunches jumped from 37 percent passing in 2001 to 78 percent in 2003.

When the district receives its grade-level test results in the fall, it divides students into quartiles by performance. Raising the percentage of students performing in the top quartile of normed tests and lowering the percentage performing in the bottom quartile has been a long-term goal of the district. Results in reading and math on the Terre Nova test indicate that the percentage of grade 8 students in the top quartiles (nationally normed at 25 percent) has grown since grade 4 from 31.9 percent to 43.8 percent in reading and from 42.1 percent to 57.3 percent in math. Likewise, the bottom quartile has decreased in reading from 11.6 percent in grade 4 to 7.8 percent in grade 8. And in math, the bottom quartile decreased from 9.9 percent to 6.6 percent. In the fall of 2003 one focused instruction school had no children (including those in special education) in the lowest quartile.

Other schools in the district are using part of the eight-step process, such as data disaggregation and regrouping of students to better meet the academic needs of their students. Their district data, said Matz, reflects these improvements.

Focused instruction has become part of the culture. Participants in a recent grade-level meeting were asked to identify a process or program that they would never want to disband, and focused instruction was their No. 1 answer.

Chapter 8

Seven Steps to Success: Struggling California School District Mines New Achievement Approaches

By Lee Simmons

In 2000 Randall-Pepper Elementary School found itself in a bind. Located in the Los Angeles suburb of Fontana, Calif., the school stood at the brink of major change. Morale among teachers and staff was low. Students were unmotivated. And the community simply was not confident that Randall-Pepper was capable of pulling itself out of such a hole.

The stagnation was a direct result of several key causes. Principal Carolyn Goode believed the school offered excuses rather than expectations for student performance. Staff was at a loss for how to implement good discipline. A lack of commitment and alignment between teachers and staff only served to heighten the antipathy, and the school failed to use student achievement data to assess the situation.

By the time Goode took over the reins in 2000, her work was cut out for her. "This school was in a high-crime, high-poverty area. We used to have a lot of graffiti on campus," Goode said.

The graffiti was a mere reflection of the discontent breeding inside the school and within the community. It was also experienced across the entire Fontana Unified School District (USD). Today, 43,000 students attend Fontana schools—almost triple the number of students 15 years ago—and 89 percent are eligible for free or reduced-priced lunches.

At Randall-Pepper and across the district, tackling the challenge of improving student performance amid such low morale and high poverty was not exactly a walk in the park. "There wasn't a lot of concern about the (achievement) gap. The expectations really weren't high for any students," said Karen Harshman, former Fontana superintendent who retired in July 2003. "We were just concerned about getting kids through and graduated, and that was it."

Fast forward three years, and 2004 paints quite a different picture. In three years Randall-Pepper exceeded state targets for increases in California's Academic Performance Index (API). Whereas 85 percent of students in the kindergarten-through-grade-5 school were below standards in reading and math, 60 percent are now meeting or exceeding standards in both.

Fontana USD—now 38 schools strong with two more under construction—recently received two awards for overall improvement: the national Dispelling the Myth Award and the All Kids All Stars Trophy, both awarded by the Education Trust (established by the American Association of Higher Education). The district has outpaced average statewide improvement for five years.

Recreating a school, not to mention an entire district, into an accurate assessor of student achievement was not an overnight phenomenon. Instead, the story of Fontana's educational facelift is a systematic, methodical peek into how ailing schools can set themselves up for continuous student achievement.

Overcoming Obstacles

To better understand Fontana's road to improved student achievement, a look back at history is necessary. Considered a rapid-growth district, Fontana counted only 16,000 students in 1986. Nearly 20 years later, that number has risen to 43,000 and steadily climbing.

For many years the district was located in the heart of a predominantly blue-collar community, home to thousands of steel workers who found employment at the Kaiser Fontana Steel Mill. After 40 years in business, the mill closed in 1983, sending hundreds of families packing to seek opportunities elsewhere. At the same time, the Fontana demographic began changing. New home construction gathered momentum throughout the mid- to late-1980s and was spurred in large part by the onset of subsidized housing.

"Multiple-dwelling housing put in by the city in the early 80s really changed the demographic," Harshman said. "Large numbers of people moved out from Los Angeles. It was affordable."

By 1990, the district was speckled with huge apartment complexes that became home to wage laborers and families living on public assistance. All the low-income, single- and multi-family developments created a destination for families subsisting well below the poverty level.

The demographic shifts of the 1980s and 1990s helped mold Fontana USD into its present incarnation: Nearly three-quarters of the school district's children are Hispanic; 11 percent are white; 9 percent are African American; and 3 percent constitute other ethnicities. Additionally, 38 percent of students speak or are learning English as a second language.

As many as 17 people live in a single-family home in Fontana, said Mike Bement, executive director of Learning Plus Associate (www.standardsplus.org). A natural result is that many students move from one school to another during a school year; some move as often as three times a year.

"Another huge factor was the density in single homes and the mobility of students from campus to campus. One campus had a 150-percent mobility rate," Bement said. "We deal with a fair number of evictions, which prompts movement between relatives' homes."

As the community began to experience a bricks-and-mortar metamorphosis, so did the traditional standards held by educators in Fontana.

Before the mid-1990s, the technology to examine and analyze achievement scores did not exist; nor did the expectation that a majority of students might go to college. "So many in the community thought our kids were going to get a job at the mill," Bement said.

In 1999 a new awareness began to evolve. It was the year that California began publishing its API, which set new standards for accountability in public schools. The federal No Child Left Behind act followed close at heel and put pressure on states to raise the bar on public grade-school education.

In 1998 the Fontana school board directed Harshman to invite an outside party to conduct an audit of the district's overall operations. The findings, released in the spring of 1999, did not paint a pretty picture. "They really said it like they thought," Harshman said of the 10-member auditing team. "All of the pimples and warts were exposed for what they were. We sort of sat there stunned."

The audit essentially found that Fontana USD was a district of independent operators. Every school operated separately and distinctly from the others, with no consistency existing among schools in program or practice. Each had its own textbooks and tests. Add to that equation the high mobility of students, and it bred a situation where moving to a neighboring school was akin to moving to a totally different school district.

The audit's final judgment boiled down to a simple problem: Current educational practices in Fontana actually impeded student learning. "That was probably the biggest 'ah-hah!'" Harshman said. "It was an eye opener and a challenge."

Such less-than-stellar reviews enabled Harshman and the district to begin building a new vision. At the direction of the school board, a district team broke down the report into several manageable pieces, each to be tackled in its own way. By scrutinizing every part of the district's operations, the team came up with 280 benchmarks (90 percent of the report's recommendations have since been met).

The vast majority of the recommendations revolved around creating an aligned curriculum and monitoring the system for student achievement. "Fontana wasn't unusual," Harshman said. "Every district in California was looking at ways to start making academic achievement the focus."

Brazosport and Beyond

Harshman first heard of the eight-step process in January 2000. Gerald Anderson, a former superintendent of the Brazosport Independent School District, gave a presentation at a conference in Monterrey, Calif. on how he and his fellow educators managed to turn around a faltering district. The Brazosport story was one in which students from impoverished and ethnically diverse backgrounds were finally performing up to par with students from wealthier backgrounds, all due to a new mindset in process improvement and the eight-step process.

Harshman not only thought this was possible in Fontana, but also believed it was absolutely necessary. After hearing Anderson speak a second time the same year (this time with a Fontana board member and the head of the teachers association attending), the school board decided to try and mold the eight-step process into a workable approach for Fontana.

The plan called for analyzing test scores, building an instructional calendar, and determining where deficits existed in student performance—all in a way that fit the Fontana USD profile. Because of the district's size as well as the influx of new teachers, Harshman was initially skeptical that teachers and staff were capable of creating their own material. So Harshman looked elsewhere to purchase materials that teachers could then use. With troubles accessing appropriate material and copyright permissions, Fontana decided to develop its own material to begin constructing its plan. Teams of teachers began developing an instructional calendar, while training was started for principals and teachers to learn how to analyze test data. The needed alignments within and among schools were beginning to take place.

The sudden burst of lesson and curriculum planning prompted the district to create the Fontana Educational Institute (recently renamed Learning Plus Associates), a nonprofit organization devoted to developing and marketing standards-based curriculum used by the district. It trademarks under Standards Plus, a federally approved curriculum enhancement program using effective schools and total quality management research.

Fontana's Standards Plus Focus on Achievement (FOA) program includes 10-minute daily mini-lessons, assessments, and maintenance activities that are aligned with California state standards and the High School Exit Exam (HSEE) standards for language arts and mathematics. Lessons (such as figures 16 and 17 on the following pages) are organized by content cluster and include scripted direct instruction that can be followed without much prior planning.

Teacher

STANDARDS PLUS™ – LANGUAGE ARTS

Content Cluster: Sentence Structure   **Level:** 3rd Grade
Focus: Complete Sentences   **Lesson:** # 1

Standard: 1.0 Written and Oral English Language Conventions.
1.1 Understand and be able to use complete and correct declarative, interrogative, imperative, and exclamatory sentences in writing and speaking. *(Prerequisite HSEE Standard)*

Introduction: Please read the following information to the students. "A sentence is a group of words that express a complete thought. Not all groups of words are sentences. To determine if a group of words is a sentence, ask these two basic questions."

Who or what someone or something is? (Does the group of words tell who someone is or what something is?)
Who or what did something? (Does the group of words tell who or what did something?)
What happened? (Does the group of words tell what happened?)

If the group of words answers those questions, it expresses a complete thought. It is a sentence. If the group of words does not answer questions, it does not express a complete thought. The group of words is a sentence fragment.

> **Example 1:**   Mr. Smith is my teacher.
> This is a complete sentence because it tells who someone is.
>
> **Example 2:**   The boys went to school.
> *Who or what did something?* (The boys)   *What happened?* (went to school.)
> This is a complete sentence because it answers the questions.
>
> **Example 3:**   Played in the pool.
> *Who or what did something?* (?)   *What happened?* (Played in the pool.)
> This is not a complete sentence. It is a sentence fragment because it does not answer the questions. It tells only part of a thought. Change the fragment into a complete sentence by adding a word or words to answer the question of *who or what.* Call on student volunteers for an example of a complete sentence.

Instructions: Read the group of words. Determine if the group of words answers the following questions: A. *Who or what did something?*, B. *What happened?*, or C. Both A and B, which indicate that the group of words is a complete sentence.

Teacher Tips: Ask students: *Who or what did something? and What happened?* during writer's workshop when student writing indicates a sentence fragment. The goal is to have students ask the same questions of themselves when writing.

Closure: "A sentence is a group of words that express a complete thought and answers the questions: *Who or what? and What happened?*"

Answers:

1. A	4. B
2. C	5. C
3. A	6. B

Figure 16

Student

STANDARDS PLUS ™ – LANGUAGE ARTS

Content Cluster: Sentence Structure   **Focus:** Complete Sentences

Standard: 1.0 Written and Oral English Language Conventions.
1.1 Understand and be able to use complete and correct declarative, interrogative, imperative, and
exclamatory sentences in writing and speaking. *(Prerequisite HSEE Standard)*

Lesson # 1

A sentence is a group of words that express a complete thought. Not all groups of words are sentences.
To determine if a group of words is a sentence, ask some basic questions.

Who or what someone or something is? (Does this group of words tell who or what something is?)
Who or what did something? (Does the group of words tell who or what did something?)
What happened? (Does the group of words tell what happened?)
A complete sentence answers these questions.

Example 1:   Mr. Smith is my teacher.
This is a complete sentence because it tells <u>who</u> <u>someone</u> <u>is</u>.

Example 2:   The boys went to school.
Who or what did something?
This is a complete sentence because it answers both questions. Who or what? (The boys)
What happened? (went to school.)

Example 3:   Played in the pool.
This is **not** a complete sentence. It is a sentence fragment because it does not answers both questions.
It tells only part of a thought. It does not have a subject. It does <u>not</u> tell how or what.

Instructions: Read the group of words. Determine if the group of words answers the following
questions: A. *Who or what? (the subject)*,   B. *What happened? (the predicate)*, or C. Circle the letter
of the correct choice. C indicates a complete sentence with a subject and predicate.

1. David and his brother.
A. Answers *Who or what?* (the subject)
B. Answers *What happened?*(the predicate)
C. Answers both A and B (the subject and predicate)

2. We drove to the mall.
A. Answers *Who or what?* (the subject)
B. Answers *What happened?*(the predicate)
C. Answers both A and B (the subject and predicate)

3. The reading teacher.
A. Answers *Who or what?* (the subject)
B. Answers *What happened?*(the predicate)
C. Answers both A and B (the subject and predicate)

4. Rides a scooter to school.
A. Answers *Who or what?* (the subject)
B. Answers *What happened?*(the predicate)
C. Answers both A and B (the subject and predicate)

5. Our dog is friendly.
A. Answers *Who or what?* (the subject)
B. Answers *What happened?*(the predicate)
C. Answers both A and B (the subject and predicate)

6. Jumped rope yesterday.
A. Answers *Who or what?* (the subject)
B. Answers *What happened?*(the predicate)
C. Answers both A and B (the subject and predicate)

Figure 16 (cont.)

STANDARDS PLUS™ – LANGUAGE ARTS

Content Cluster: Sentence Structure	Level: 9th/10th Grade
Focus: Awkward Construction	Lesson: #1

California Language Arts Content Standard and *High School Exit Exam Standard*: Writing Strategies, *Organization and Focus* 1.1 Establish controlling impression or coherent thesis that conveys a clear and distinctive perspective on the subject and maintain a consistent tone and focus throughout the piece of writing. Written and Oral English language Conventions, *Grammar and Mechanics of Writing* 1.3 Demonstrate an understanding of proper English usage and control of grammar, paragraph and sentence structure, diction, and syntax. (Grades 9 and 10)

Introduction:

This next ten-day unit addresses sentence structure. It includes awkward construction, fragments, misplaced modifiers, run-ons, parallel structure, and redundancy. Some of these categories spill over into each other, but we'll make an attempt to keep them separate. Today's lesson deals with awkward construction.

Instruction:

Read through the Lesson number 1 text on the student sheet. Stress logic and clarity. As you work through the three exercises, point out how the incorrect answers are confusing, unclear, or redundant. Often, the best version may also be the shortest version. (See sentence number 3.) Discuss the choices with the class.

Answers:
1. B
2. D
3. B

Figure 17

Name:_____

STANDARDS PLUS™ – LANGUAGE ARTS

Content Cluster: Sentence Structure   Focus: Awkward Construction

Lesson #1

In order for a sentence to clearly express an idea or a sequence of ideas, it must be clearly written, with the words in logical order. Subjects usually come before verbs, and modifiers need to be placed logically near the words they modify. This kind of sentence construction calls for a good eye and a good ear. After you've written a sentence, see if it looks right and see if it sounds right. If the sentence is not clear, or if it is confusing, rearrange the words so they make better sense. The more you practice, the easier it becomes. Learn to trust your ear. Read the sentence aloud. See if it sounds right and the idea is clear.

Practice

Read each sentence below. There may be a mistake in sentence structure. If you find a mistake, choose the answer that is written most clearly and correctly. If there is no mistake, choose "Correct as is."

1. Sarah, my sister, is the youngest of my brothers and sisters.

   A. Of all my brothers and sisters, Sarah is the oldest sister.
   B. Sarah is the oldest of my brothers and sisters.
   C. My sister Sara is the oldest sister of my brothers and sisters.
   D. Correct as is

2. Explaining his actions, John tried desperately to make them understand his reasons for what he had done.

   A. John tried desperately to make them understand, explaining his actions, his reasons for what he had done.
   B. John tried desperately to make them understand his reasons for what he had done explaing his actions.
   C. Explaining his actions, trying desperately to make them understand his reasons for what he had done, was John.
   D. Correct as is

3. Inside the closet was Tracy, looking for her earrings she had lost.

   A. Losing her earrings caused Tracy to look in the closet.
   B. Tracy was looking in the closet for her lost earrings.
   C. Tracy, in the closet, looking for her earrings, was there.
   D. Correct as is

Figure 17 (cont.)

In breaking down the eight-step process for its own uses, the district made a few key modifications. Teachers decided to combine tutoring and enrichment under the same step, thereby creating a seven-step process for Fontana:

1. data analysis;
2. development of a calendar;
3. instructional focus through mini-lessons;
4. weekly assessment of students;
5. reteach, review, and enrichment;
6. ongoing maintenance of learned material; and
7. monitoring.

Under the "plan" portion of the process, teachers and principals analyze data and develop a lesson calendar. The "do" portion involves teaching lessons to students, maintaining what is learned, and reinforcing lessons at a later date. The "check" part includes assessments and monitoring of classrooms by principals. And the "act" portion involves re-teaching when necessary.

This Standards Plus plan created a school-wide focus by providing students with structure, giving teachers instructional tools, removing the fear factor from process improvement, and eliminating excuses. More than 2,000 Standards Plus math and language arts mini-lessons, which require 10 to 15 minutes of classroom time, have been written. Lessons are given every Monday through Thursday, with each aligned to a specific California standard. Students are taught specific elements of each standard up to five times.

Alongside Standards Plus came a change in the high school graduation requirements for seniors. Harshman managed to change the requirements so that the default curriculum for all students, regardless of anything, was the University of California A-to-G requirements. In other words, students were required to take and pass the classes needed to be admitted to the university, regardless of whether they intended to go on with their studies.

Only the third district in the state to adopt that policy, Harshman said she believes it will make a huge difference in raising achievement standards among high school students.

"To succeed in the work force, you need the same skill set that you need to succeed in college," Bement added.

Another obstacle the district has surmounted is the training of principals in data analysis. Actually mandating structured time in the work day to read and discuss student performance research has taken the pressure off principals to balance that with the business of managing a school, not to mention improved morale among the district's principals.

With Fontana teachers now writing all the curriculum guides, assessments, and focus lessons, the first area they aligned was math. The district's multiyear growth pattern in math is a good example of how the addition of mini-lessons and Fontana's other reforms helped spur overall academic improvement.

In 1994 Fontana USD mandated a new math curriculum for all elementary teachers. The plan met with contention among teachers, many of whom continued to use their old textbooks and forced students to hide them whenever administrators entered the classroom. The same year, the district created an educational accountability department that began developing teacher-driven trimester assessments. But test results were use to illustrate how important the new curriculum was. "Until this time, we had only random patterns in achievement scores," Bement said. "We self-administered the ITBS (Iowa Tests of Basic Skills) at several schools, but we really wanted to develop data which we could use formatively. From that point forward, math scores district wide consistently rose each year for the next nine years."

In 1999 Fontana identified 23 schools as program improvement campuses under Title 1 mandates for improving low-performing schools. As of March 2004, the district counted only five such program-improvement schools.

Perhaps the most progress in Fontana can be seen in the district's scores on the state's API (Figure 18, page 128). California rates individual school achievement based on compiled test scores. The API ranges from 200 to 1,000, with 800 and above considered the goal for all schools in the state.

In 1999 Fontana's elementary schools averaged 493 on the API. Five years later, the same schools averaged 652. Middle schools

Fontana District Scores on the California API

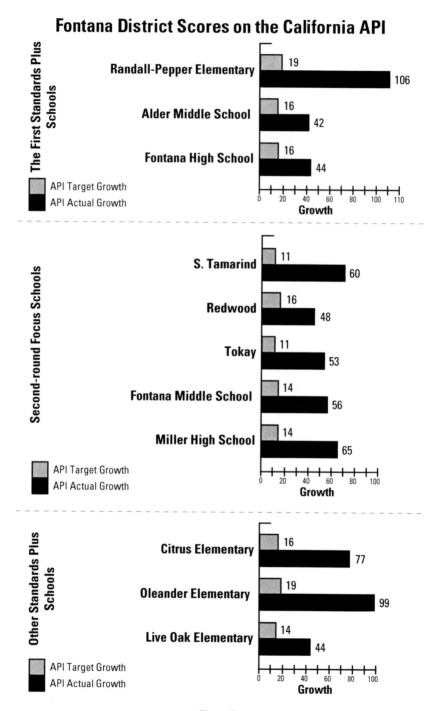

Figure 18

averaged 512 in 1999 and have since climbed to 619 as of early 2004. And high schools, averaging 496 in 1999, marked a 601 average on the index in early 2004.

Although the scores still have yet to meet the state goals, Fontana educators say they represent significant steps forward when compared to average increases for schools across the state. For instance, statewide, high schools rose from 622 to 662 over a four-year period, 40-point difference. In Fontana, high schools rose 105 points over the same period.

"We're still far from where we want to be, but we're much closer," said Bement.

Randall-Pepper's Leap Ahead

Randall-Pepper Elementary showed the largest gains of any school in the district. With 85 percent of the school community speaking a language other than English, and 61 percent of the student body considered English language learners, the instructional focus at Randall-Pepper has had to give equal access to every population in the school.

And ensuring equal access to all students means getting all staff on the same page.

"We try to identify the needs of students but also get implications for our professional development for teachers and staff," Principal Goode said. "In this process, we include the total school. Our mission is learning for all."

Prior to Goode's tenure, many teachers and staff at the school had their hands full maintaining discipline. The school was additionally plagued by a lack of commitment and alignment among teachers and staff, which only compounded the sense of antipathy on the campus.

The problems were answered in part by the creation of grade-level teams, in which teachers from each grade share assessment data with colleagues. This sharing of data helped teachers get a better handle on what their students' needs were and helped enforce a disciplined classroom environment.

In addition, Goode started breaking down staff meetings into grade-level group meetings so that teachers could explore new ways of accomplishing the seven-step process. Initially, the biggest challenge to implementing the process lay in professional development, Goode said. Teachers had not previously had opportunities to work with this kind of data.

In turn, the challenge created an opportunity in helping staff believe that all children could learn, no matter what their particular circumstances are. Karen Bush, a second-grade teacher at Randall-Pepper, said Goode's supervision and insistence on a team approach that includes all staff helped pave the way toward a more unified approach.

"A major piece of this entire process is believing that if you implement all of the steps, children will achieve," Goode added. "Success breeds success." Getting teachers committed to the process was a matter of organizing scheduled time for them. When Goode or another administrator sees a gap or need in a classroom, time is built into the teacher's schedule so that it is properly addressed. Oftentimes gaps are addressed through team meetings among teachers. Team leaders are also designated at every grade level to help keep teachers on track and accountable in their weekly language arts and math lessons and assessments.

Keeping teachers aligned within a grade level was an early challenge Goode insisted on addressing. Randall-Pepper staff began using a calendar of needs as an alignment tool. Because different schools in the district operate on different schedules, the district created this instructional calendar to help keep each school—and each grade level—focused on a week's worth of lesson plans. Each week listed on the calendar includes specific state standards that must be taught.

Bush said the calendar helps the school not only plan, but also assess how its different student subgroups are performing. "I could go to the calendar and find out what focus I should have for a week. There is one for language arts and one for math," Bush said.

Bush, who keeps statistics for the school on Standards Plus assessments, compiles a list of all the assessments made by every teacher weekly and then makes hard copies of the list available to staff. So, for instance, grade 5 language arts teachers can look at the list to find context clues for how their students performed for one week and decide whether they need to meet as a team and discuss the statistics or whether further administration support is needed in improving their students' performance.

And on Friday, teachers assess what students retained from the week's mini-lessons by giving a four-question test. The assessment usually answers at least one of four questions for a teacher: Do they need to be taught again? Should part of a lesson be reviewed? Did they master a standard? Are they ready for enrichment?

Students are separated into groups depending on how many questions they answered correctly on the weekly assessment test. Those who answered all four correctly attend a short enrichment class on Wednesday of the following week with one teacher, usually lasting 40 to 50 minutes. Those students who answered three questions attend a review with another teacher. Students who scored lower or did not pass also break off into a class with yet another teacher for remediation.

Remediation classes will occasionally include a bilingual teacher to assist English language learners. If a lesson must be retaught, Bush said, then she usually tries to present it in a different way than she did in the original lesson.

Regular maintenance is also an important part of Randall-Pepper's approach to continuous improvement. For instance, if a lesson on capitalization and punctuation is taught in September, then a teacher should reinforce those standards in January. Maintenance lessons are taught for review purposes and are typically used: after a content cluster is introduced, when concepts are difficult to introduce (such as before Christmas or spring break), as homework, or any time a teacher feels that review is needed.

The monitoring principal is a crucial part of the process, said Goode, who checks regularly on teacher pacing and whether standards are being taught. She also sets up teacher-student conferences to enable teachers to discuss a student's progress outside of the classroom when necessary and meets individually with teachers to review their data.

The plan does not end off-campus. Goode said the school arranges meetings with parents to teach them the same standards and strategies for helping their kids at home with the material. Teachers even meet parents in their homes to help ensure that a student's learning continues outside school.

"If our parents are Spanish speaking only, they don't always understand or the children don't communicate well what it is they have to do for homework," Bush said. "We get a real picture of what the child is dealing with or how much the parents are interested. Often, we find it's just a communication problem with the parent."

With grant money provided by the Nell Soto Program, teachers in Fontana are able to provide extra written materials to parents to help them assist their children with learning outside of the classroom. The district has also brought parents in for special training sessions on how to help their children with their homework, how to support their reading, how to read to them, and other topics.

API: the Initial Test

Implemented during the 2000 to 2001 school year, Fontana USD's continuous improvement methods have borne fruit in the form of rising API results. That year, the state gave Randall-Pepper a goal of increasing 19 points on the API. The school rose 106 points for a score of 535. The following year, the growth target was 552; the school scored 588.

And for the 2002 to 2003 school year, when the state asked for 599, the school posted a score of 653. Because of its success, Randall-Pepper is no longer listed as a Title 1 improvement school. And if it keeps up its current rate of achievement growth, it could surpass 700 for the 2003 to 2004 school year and meet state goals by 2006.

"Self esteem has improved," Goode said. "When you walk into classrooms, you cannot tell which students are English language learners or special needs students from others."

Harshman minces no words when identifying the main obstacles to implementing Fontana's improvement model: "Time and energy."

"I refuse to say money," she added. "It's no secret that education can use more money. If you have your priorities right, you choose how to spend your money."

Other challenges exist, such as personnel turnover and training staff and parents to understand the process. Friction tends to run high among some district administrators, said Bement, as the amount of available "institutional memory" runs out.

For instance, the district hired a new superintendent and educational services associate superintendent during the past year. Interim employees are currently handling duties in human resources and business. A supplemental retirement plan is additionally leading to several more retirements.

Questioning from the local teachers union has also added some strain, Bement said. "There was also a shift in teacher union leadership, which has brought a new negative tone and active campaigns against curriculum leadership and formal accountability measures. Our scores are going up because our teachers work so hard, they cry, 'Not because of anything the district did.' Of course, this slanders teachers who worked hard for decades with only isolated, non-systematic successes."

Bement added that the greatest staff buy-in comes when teachers begin to see their students and peers become successful. Students often start to notice the difference at week 12 each year, when they finally get proficient at the standards-based mini-lessons, Bement said.

"The parents also see relevant student performance data at parent-teacher conferences, and they see the macro-level success of thousands of English language learners achieving proficiency and of hundreds of students now achieving at grade level for the first time in recent memory," he said.

Perhaps the biggest administrative challenge lies in convincing all parties that the process has no end. "This whole process was built on continuous improvement," Harshman said. "You're never going to reach the top."

For Goode, the process helps her to keep her momentum and focus on student achievement. "It makes it easier because you're constantly planning and working toward achieving that plan," she said. "If it didn't work, you can see it immediately. There's nothing that you're waiting for."

.

Chapter 9

Combined Continuous Improvement Efforts Yield Results for South Carolina District

By Emma Skogstad

The Horry County School District in South Carolina has used an innovative combination of approaches to overcome challenges in standardized testing, early student learning, new-teacher training, and parent involvement with practices that other districts and schools can replicate.

The district is committed to improving the education standards of the nearly 30,000 students in this racially and economically diverse district and to achieving continuous, sustained performance on statewide testing. In 1992 the district began its strategic planning process in an effort to encourage teachers and community members to collaborate in making important decisions about the county's schools. The district's most recent strategic plan was implemented in November 2000. The plan, which is posted on the school district's Web site, guarantees that all students will be fully prepared, successful contributors in a rapidly changing global society through the aggressive pursuit of personalized, achievement-based, and student-centered teaching and learning.

Brenda Tanner, the chief academic officer for the Horry County School District, enumerated the many challenges involved in achieving this goal, as well as the innovative plans and strategies the district has implemented to reach its goals.

Challenges in Preparing Students for State Assessment

The Horry County School District has faced several challenges in preparing its students for state assessments. First, the results of the current South Carolina state student assessment, PACT (Palmetto Achievement Challenge Tests), provide the district with limited information about students' performance. Students receive general information in the form of a rating: below basic 1, below basic 2, basic, proficient, and advanced. This information does not give teachers information to help impact daily instruction, nor does it give the district enough information to make necessary adjustments to the curriculum. These ratings do provide information across grade levels; for example, the results will indicate that fifth graders are doing better in math than in English/language arts. But according to Tanner, "You cannot get inside that data to work with it programmatically. For example, you would not be able to tell if a child had problems with specific skills, such as reading comprehension or language use. This makes conferencing with parents challenging because there is nothing broken down to give information on an individual performance level. Teachers can tell parents that their child is scoring at a basic level in mathematics, but they can't provide feedback about specific areas where improvement is needed, such as geometry."

Another challenge of state assessment is that in grades 3 through 8, only one-third of the standards are assessed each year. Unfortunately, teachers can have no idea of which standards will be tested and therefore cannot cater instruction based on students' results from the last year. Once again, there is no way to determine which standards or areas are difficult for students. Tom Pritchard, director of the office of accountability services in Horry County, said, "A teacher compared the work she did throughout the school year to a bowling match where someone had covered the pins with a blanket. She couldn't see the pins, so she just kept throwing the ball, over and over, knowing that by July [after the statewide assessments had been scored], she'd find out what happened. As she said, there was no way to know how to correct herself."

A third challenge the school district faced in preparing students for state assessments was that in the high school, there was a delay between the time the state implemented state standards and the time the state tested students on those standards. Although students' curriculum was catered to standards, they were still being tested with a grade 10 exit exam of basic skills test (BSAP; the Basic Skills Assessment Program) in English/language arts and math. As of spring 2004, a new test called HSAP (the High School Assessment Program) should resolve the disparity between standards and assessment. The HSAP is the new grade 10 exit exam, which tests English/language arts and math and is aligned with the state standards. (The 2003 to 2004 school year was the field test for this new assessment.) Students must pass this test for graduation in South Carolina. They may be promoted to the next grade without passing the test (promotion is determined by the number of units achieved); however, they will have to retake the test in grade 11.

A fourth challenge, which Tanner described as an "instructional challenge" as far as preparing students for assessment, is the gradual budget cuts taking place at the state and local level. Additional services, such as summer school and tutoring, are still offered, but there may be fewer classes or tutoring sessions available as budgets decrease. For many years, the district has believed in the importance of its plan-do-study-act instructional cycle, which is to regularly examine what works and focus on continuous improvement. With fewer resources at hand, Tanner said, the district has had to pay even more attention to this process and to determining priorities.

Getting to Students Early

According to Tanner, the school district has developed a comprehensive plan to address the challenges faced in preparing students for statewide assessment. First, the district has implemented instructional models in language arts and mathematics that have provided a framework for instruction that has made it consistent across the district. Second is the district's emphasis on the early identification of needs and addressing those needs as soon as possible in a student's career. The district goes about this through its extensive child development program for four-year-olds. After Horry County began collecting data on different programs in 1996, district administrators realized that at-risk four-year-olds enrolled in the district's own academic program scored higher in reading, math, and writing in first, second, and third grades than students participating in preschool programs sponsored by other government agencies. By the third grade, 75 percent of the students who attended the district's preschool program scored higher than any other group of students in reading and writing.

Horry County's child development program for four-year-olds has an application and screening process with established criteria for entrance. One way that the district screens these children is through DIAL-3 (Development Indicators for the Assessment of Learning, third edition) assessments. DIAL-3 assesses children's motor, conceptualization, and language skills, as well as their skills in self-help (personal care skills such as dressing, eating, and grooming) and social development (social skills with other children and parents, including the ability to follow rules). After taking DIAL-3, students receive percentile ranks and standard scores. According to Cindy Ambrose, the executive director of elementary schools in Horry County, "We also utilize the factors associated with children being at-risk for academic difficulty:

- the mother's age at first child's birth,
- the mother's socio-economic level,
- the mother's educational level, [and]
- whether the child lives in a single- or two-parent home."

These criteria are used to award points, which are factored in along with the results of the DIAL-3. The more points a student scores, the greater his or her academic need is considered to be. After this scoring has taken place, all the children who have been screened are placed in order in terms of need. "We pick up the children with the greatest need first when we are accepting children into the program to make up the classes," said Ambrose.

These four-year-olds considered most at-need are invited to join the all-day program. The district currently serves 600 four-year-old students, about one quarter of the four-year-olds in the system. According to Ambrose, the state of South Carolina provides funding to serve about 400 children in a half-day program.

"The district has collected data on this program since 1996," said Ambrose. "The first group of students we began tracking is now in our fifth grade. Our data have consistently shown that our children served in the four-year-old program perform at the district average even though these children are identified as the most at-risk when they are accepted into the program."

She went on to say that the children who are now most at-risk on entry in the district's kindergarten program are the children who are not served in the child development program, Head Start, or private child care centers. "Our child development students are often our strongest kindergarten students," she said.

The program has been so popular that more students apply and qualify than the district can accommodate. "Because of the results we have, the school board has made it a priority to expand the program and serve all children who are identified for services," said Ambrose. "We use Title I funding to offer the full-day program, and currently five of the classes are totally paid for through local funds. We have 30 classes across the district. During the 2004 through 2005 school year, the board hopes to add classes to serve 200 more children."

According to Tanner, the district works hard to focus on intervention, especially on trying to get to students at an early age. Programs such as this one with four-year-olds are designed to help students based on needs. To help students, Tanner said, "intervention and prevention must be a priority."

Using Computer-based Assessments

To address the diagnostic limitations of the South Carolina state assessment results, the Horry County School District piloted a computerized assessment system developed by a nonprofit assessment organization, the Northwest Evaluation Association (NWEA). The name of the assessment system is Measures of Academic Progress (MAP). After two years of investigating the MAP system and talking to other school districts about its effectiveness, Horry County Schools piloted the MAP assessment in spring 2003. MAP was piloted in 11 schools: eight elementary schools, two middle schools, and one high school. The results of the pilot was overwhelmingly positive. Teachers and administrators were particularly impressed by how the results of the assessment would inform their instructional program. During the 2003 to 2004 school year, the MAP assessment was implemented district wide, in all 45 district schools, grades 2 through 10.

The MAP assessments are administered in September, December, and March in reading, language usage, and mathematics. The computer-based program allows teachers, principals, and administrators to get results immediately and to use the results to attain important diagnostic information about the students. These results can be used to monitor progress throughout the year and to adapt instruction to provide additional instruction where students need it.

MAP is an computerized adaptive testing system. Students at each grade level enter the test a their grade level, and then the test adjusts its level based on their responses; it levels down for students who miss too many questions or up for students who get a certain number of questions in a row correct. As the test progresses, each student receive a unique test developed especially for him or her. The emphasis is on a learning continuum, and the test results provide detailed information about students' skills and concepts. In addition to the exit exam given in grade 10, South Carolina currently tests mathematics, English/language arts, science, and social studies in grades 3 through 8, with multiple-choice, extended response, and open-ended questions. MAP tests are used in grades 2 through 10 in language arts, reading, and math. Tanner said that the district will consider using science and social studies MAP tests in the future, but no definite plans have yet been established.

After students take the MAP tests, teachers, principals, and administrators receive computer spreadsheets of students' results. These results have been analyzed by the system, and they provide very detailed information of student achievement. Tanner said, "The results allow you to know strengths and weaknesses" in a way not provided by the state assessment results. The MAP tests are also nationally normed, meaning they provide information not only about individual students but also about how the results of students in Horry County compare to national results.

According to Tom Pritchard, director of the Office of Accountability Services in Horry County, working with the NWEA is extremely cost effective for the school district. In the 2003 to 2004 school year, the cost was $5.25 per student for three assessments, including reports with data and analysis. In the 2004 to 2005 school year, this price raised to $6.00 per student. The school district spent four days holding two two-day workshops with NWEA trainers. Curriculum specialists, teachers, and principals were all trained on how to interpret and use the MAP data received for each student.

Tanner said, this information is invaluable. In the past, the district had to rely on teacher assessment for information about student achievement, and unfortunately, this assessment would vary from teacher to teacher. Now, the MAP data can be used to pinpoint students' achievement. "This affects the types of services we provide students," said Tanner. She pointed out that students who do well may need extra opportunities, whereas students who do poorly will need additional tutoring and information to bring them up to speed. Using the results from these tests, the district works with teachers to provide flexible instruction for different skill areas. As discussed in the next section, this ability to see students' specific strengths and weaknesses has changed the way instruction is presented in Horry County Schools.

Flexible Instruction

The Horry County School District worked with APQC from 2002 to 2004 to reinforce the need for planning, implementing, and studying best practices and to look at ways to overcome the challenges of assessment and standards-based instruction. APQC encouraged teachers to develop team time (also called "focus time"), which is additional time in the day that could be used to focus on specific skills that need attention. Representatives from APQC worked with the district to help teachers identify areas where students needed more support. As previously discussed, there was initially no way for teachers to know which standards students needed additional help on; statewide test results simply did not provide this information. Initially, teachers worked on using their own internal assessments to develop team time. Now that teachers have access to MAP results three times per year, they can use these results to help them with time and scheduling.

With "focus time" in mind, schools in the Horry County School District developed flexible grouping, where students are temporarily regrouped during the day according to their instructional needs. During this focus time, selected standards are taught.

For example, all grade 4 classes might have focus time at the same time during the day. The classes would group at this time according to the identified needs of the students. Some students might focus on learning cause and effect, and others might learn about the elements of a plot. The focus is on students' mastery of skills; teachers decide how long each group will stay together and may provide a mini-assessment at the end of a week to determine mastery. They may decide to continue for another week, or they may regroup students so they can learn a new topic. Tanner stressed the importance of monitoring student growth individually. Teachers must know which students still need help at the end of the group time and provide additional help to these students until mastery has occurred. This type of flexible scheduling has allowed Horry District to move from teaching all students in grade levels the same content to identifying needs and using flexible grouping to emphasize the content students have the most trouble grasping.

Instructional Experts

Another way that Horry County has addressed the need for assessment improvement is through the use of curriculum specialists, otherwise known as "instructional coaches." Curriculum specialists have been teachers at one time, but they are no longer assigned to a classroom. Instead, they instruct teachers on coaching assessment and help teachers analyze student test results. They meet with teachers for professional development. In addition, district learning specialists work in the schools with teachers on a daily basis. They go to many different schools and do similar tasks to curriculum specialists. Previously, the district gave content specialists equal time at each school, but now it looks at students' achievement results to schedule the content specialists' time. This means that some higher performing schools will likely not see the specialists as often as lower performing schools, where the need for assessment help is greater.

Content specialists are tasked with being experts on standards, assessment, text books, and state programs and initiatives. They do a lot of training. For example, teachers at a school might identify a need in working with students. They would schedule an appointment with a learning specialist, who would go to the school and meet with the teachers to present information. There would be dialogue and follow-up. Specialists also work with lead teachers and curriculum specialists to share information about instructional strategies and state assessment.

The Horry County Assessment Center

From an administrative perspective, Tanner counts the district's assessment center among its best practices. Run by Pritchard, the center's director, the center provides detailed information on student achievement results by facilitating data analysis. Annually, the center provides principals with information, such as with pie charts that show results over several years and data on groupings of students (figures 19 and 20, pages 152-157).

The center also refines data so that it is not overwhelming for teachers, principals, and administrators; it also gives information on how to manage and use the data. The refined data helps administrators to analyze achievement and plan future initiatives.

The center provides large notebooks in the fall that include information based on the May state assessments. According to Pritchard, the district maintains three years' worth of data in the notebook. In addition to the total group, there is a breakdown by ethnicity, as well as by eligibility for free or reduced lunches to measure the impact of economic indicators.

According to Pritchard, the center is eagerly awaiting August 2004, when it will have data on the impact of three-time-per-year MAP testing on students' statewide assessment scores. However, Pritchard noted that a student's MAP RIT scores (RIT stands for Rausch Unit) reflect the level at which a student is currently performing, unrelated to his or her age or grade level. This score can help administrators predict with great accuracy whether the child will

Grade Six 2000-2003 PACT Test Results

Percentage of Students at Each Level in Mathematics for 2000

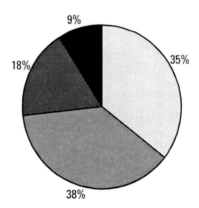

9%

18%

35%

38%

Below Basic
Basic
Proficient
Advanced

Percentage of Students at Each Level in Mathematics for 2001

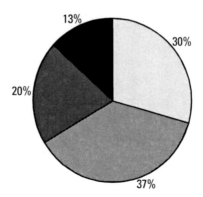

13%

30%

20%

37%

Below Basic
Basic
Proficient
Advanced

Figure 19

Grade Six 2000-2003 PACT Test Results

Percentage of Students at Each Level in Mathematics for 2002

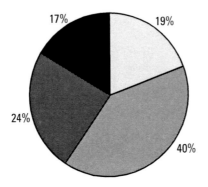

- ☐ Below Basic
- Basic
- Proficient
- ■ Advanced

Percentage of Students at Each Level in Mathematics for 2003

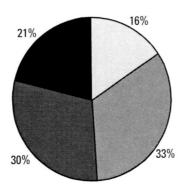

- ☐ Below Basic
- Basic
- Proficient
- ■ Advanced

Figure 19 (cont.)

2000-2003 PACT Results by Ethnicity

Percentage of African American Students
at Each Level in Mathematics for 2000

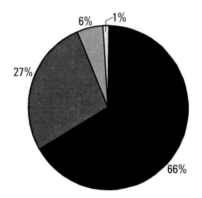

Below Basic
Basic
Proficient
Advanced

Percentage of White Students at Each Level
in Mathematics for 2000

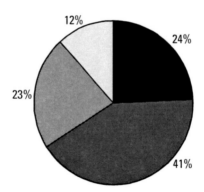

Below Basic
Basic
Proficient
Advanced

Figure 20

2000-2003 PACT Results by Ethnicity

Percentage of African American Students
at Each Level in Mathematics for 2001

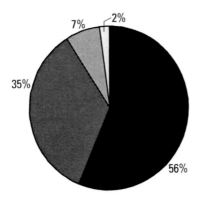

Below Basic
Basic
Proficient
Advanced

Percentage of White Students at Each Level
in Mathematics for 2001

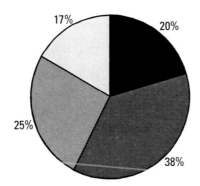

Below Basic
Basic
Proficient
Advanced

Figure 20 (cont.)

2000-2003 PACT Results by Ethnicity

Percentage of African American Students at Each Level in Mathematics for 2002

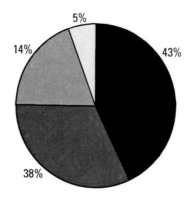

Below Basic
Basic
Proficient
Advanced

Percentage of White Students at Each Level in Mathematics for 2002

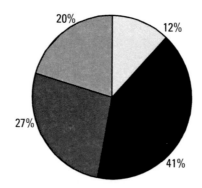

Below Basic
Basic
Proficient
Advanced

Figure 20 (cont.)

2000-2003 PACT Results by Ethnicity

Percentage of African American Students at Each Level in Mathematics for 2003

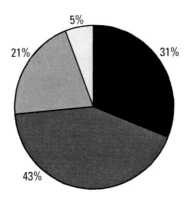

Below Basic
Basic
Proficient
Advanced

Percentage of White Students at Each Level in Mathematics for 2003

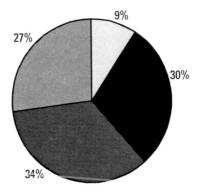

Below Basic
Basic
Proficient
Advanced

Figure 20 (cont.)

fall in the below basic, basic, proficient, or advanced category of the statewide assessment. The MAP test results also give administrators a scale by which to measure a student's growth over time, similarly to how parents measure their young children's physical growth with a pencil mark on the door jam. Because the three tests are given by March of the school year, teachers have plenty of time to prepare students for the May statewide assessments.

Pritchard works with the technology department to access, post, and manage information in different ways. He noted that he and his team work closely in the same division at IT and that a lot of their information is available online. Because of the sensitivity of the data, it is password protected, with every teacher and principal having access. In addition, information is posted on the Horry County Web site, where a lot of data about students is available for parents or others interested in seeing how the district is performing. For example, the Horry County School District's online progress report, updated in May 2004, shows how schools are working toward performance goals enumerated in the strategic plan. A section of this report follows (Figure 21).

"First in Five"

"First in Five" expresses Horry County School District's commitment to excellence. According to Tanner, First in Five was established as a vision for the district; the vision states that "Horry County Schools will be the state's top-performing school district in student achievement by 2005."

In 2003, 86 percent of the district's schools received an "excellent" or "good" rating on its state report card, as opposed to only 52 percent of schools statewide. Horry County School District was one of only nine of the state's 85 districts to receive a state report card absolute rating of excellent for last year's student achievement. Of the 21 "districts like ours," Horry County School District was the only one to receive an excellent rating. "Districts like ours" compares districts with similar demographics.

The First in Five vision is clearly articulated on Horry County School District's Web site, where in addition to the mission statement, strategies for meeting goals are clearly outlined.

Figure 21 – Portion of "First In Five" Performance Report—May 2004

Long-range Performance Goals	Four-year Performance				Change from last year	Change over 2 years
	Status (2000)	Status (2001)	Status (2002)	Status (2003)		
1. 90% of all students will attain a text reading level "3" or above by the end of kindergarten.	77%	89.4%	92.8%	96.2%	+3.4	+6.8
2. 90% of students will attain a text reading level above "16" by the end of first grade.	75%	81.4%	86.9%	90.9%	+4.0	+9.5
10. The percentage of students in grade 4 who meet state and local standards in mathematics will increase to at least 90%.	66.2%	74.5%	84.4%	89.7%	+5.3	+15.2
12. The percentage of students in grade 5 who meet state and local standards in mathematics will increase to at least 90%.	62.5%	69.3%	82.0%	87.6%	+5.6	+18.3
14. The percentage of students in grade 6 who meet state and local standards in mathematics will increase to at least 90%.	64.8%	70.4%	78.3%	82.5%	+4.2	+12.1
22. The percentage of students in grade 4 who score "advanced" on PACT mathematics will increase by 15%.	8.7%	16.2%	25.9%	26.7%	+0.6	+10.5
46. All students in grade 8 will be proficient in mathematics by 2014.	NA	NA	29.2%	27.4%	-1.8	NA
48. At least 30% of graduates will successfully complete at least one advanced placement, International Baccalaureate, or college credit course.	25%	25%	32%	26%	-6	+1
49. The average SAT score (combined math and verbal) for high school students will be equal to the national average.	978	993	1009	1031	+22	+38

Figure 21 (cont.) – Portion of "First In Five" Performance Report—May 2004

Long-range Performance Goals	Four-year Performance				Change from last year	Change over 2 years
	Status (2000)	Status (2001)	Status (2002)	Status (2003)		
51. The percentage of students in grade 10 who score at or above the state standard in mathematics on the exit exam "first try" will increase to 90%.	74.7%	81.4%	82.6%	85.3%	+2.7	+2.9
55. The number of students with disabilities who earn a state diploma or Horry County Individualized Diploma will increase to 60%.	46	52	46	54	+8.0	+2.0
56. At least 30% of graduates will qualify for LIFE scholarships, meeting both grade point average and SAT/ACT criteria established by the state, by 2004.	18.5%	18.6%	22.3%	14.3%	*Eligibility criterion raised in 2003	*Eligibility criterion raised in 2003
57. The percentage of parents/guardians who participate in a personalized learning plan conference will increase each year, with at least 96% of parents at all grade levels (elementary, middle, and high) attending.	E: 98% M: 95% H: 71%	89.8%	94.4%	98.3%	+3.9	+8.5
63. The number of teachers attaining National Board Certification will increase to 75.	4	28	62	82	+20	+78
64. At least 85% of students (S), parents (P), and teachers (T) surveyed will indicate that they feel safe at school.	S: 70% P: 84% T: 81%	S: 79.5% P: 84.3% T: 96.1%	S: 78.2% P: 87.2% T: 94.0%	S: 88.9% P: 88.7% T: 98.2%	S: +10.7 P: +1.5 T: +4.2	S: +9.4 P: +4.4 T: +0.1
65. Each year, the district as a whole will have a .10-gain in the Absolute rating until "Excellent" is attained.	NA	Good	Good	Excellent	+1 level	+1 level
66. Each year, the district as a whole will have a .10-gain in the Improvement rating until "Excellent" is attained.	NA	Below Average	Average	Average	+0.1	+1 level

Figure 21 (cont.) – Portion of "First In Five" Performance Report—May 2004		
Summary (as of May 3, 2004)	Number	Percentage
Goals that have shown progress during most recent two-year period	36	75%
Goals that have not shown progress during most recent two-year period	10	21%
No change	2	4%
Summary (as of May 3, 2004)	Number	Percentage
Goals that have shown progress during most recent one-year period	44	67%
Goals that have not shown progress during most recent one-year period	22	33%
No change	0	0%

These strategies follow.

1. Implement a standards-based system that aligns curriculum, instruction, and assessment.
2. Personalize education for each student.
3. Ensure system effectiveness and accountability.
4. Energize and integrate all resources of the diverse community into full support of the mission and objectives.
5. Create and sustain a safe environment conducive to learning.
6. Ensure the involvement of families in the education of each student.
7. Ensure that the educational community is free from racial and cultural bias.
8. Develop and implement a comprehensive, long-range facilities plan to support the mission and objectives.
9. Acquire the necessary funds to achieve the mission and objectives.

Tanner said, "[First in Five] is not about a label or an award. It is about providing opportunities for students to perform at the highest level possible." Like other successful initiatives in Horry County School District, articulating the vision, in Tanner's opinion, helps to provide focus and raises awareness in the total community, as well as in the educational community.

Chapter 10

Radical Culture Shift Injects Winning Academic Spirit at Iowa High School

By Becki Hack

What if high schools held pep rallies for nationally standardized tests? What if every student received individual attention from a mentor? What if those mentors reviewed test results one-on-one and offered help to improve? What if students could understand "the big picture" and truly perceive testing as important now and in the future? Questions like these churned still waters at Muscatine High School in Muscatine, Iowa and created significant change.

Faced with low test scores as well as socioeconomic and racial performance gaps, Muscatine High School looked to its district's elementary and middle schools that had survived similar storms by radically altering their course: change the belief system. Wary at first, Muscatine High School soon found that believing every child can improve and implementing the eight-step process, created by the Brazosport Independent School District, works in any school—even a high school.

When educators focused individualized attention on every child, believed each student is capable of greater performance, created the academic process to enable individual learning, explained and reinforced the importance of tests, and demonstrated their commitment, students connected. They rose to the challenge. Along with their teachers and administrators, these high school students found an enthusiasm and excitement for academics like never before.

New Ideas

High school educators know their culture is unique. After all, their "kids" are verging on young adults whose worlds have boundaries much larger than school or education; their time is divided among many competing activities. The environment is rarely as openly nurturing as that of an elementary. Gaps in previous curricula are difficult to remedy. Too many students step through the doors poorly prepared, for various reasons, and have apathy toward hurdling these barriers. These are excuses, maybe, but they are obstacles nonetheless. That "difference" was reason enough for Muscatine High School to at first disregard elementary and middle school initiatives focused on the eight-step process. It soon witnessed results that sparked a new way of thinking.

Sitting on the banks of the Mississippi River in southeastern Iowa, Muscatine Community School District comprises nine elementary schools, two middle schools, and one high school. Its mission is to ensure excellence in education for every student. Jane Evans, the district's director of educational services, launched her school's renewed effort to accomplish that mission through a chance meeting with Pat Davenport, a former Brazosport administrator.

Muscatine Community School District is part of Mississippi Bend Area Education Agency, an intermediate unit that serves 22 public and 21 private Iowa school districts. Through one of the Mississippi Bend AEA staff development meetings, Evans met Davenport and became enthralled with the eight-step process. "I was so impressed with the process because it is down to earth, logical, inexpensive, and what good teachers have been doing forever: looking at data, making modifications to instruction, and making sure all students learn. This was just a systematic way of boosting student achievement."

Eager to take action, Evans requested district Superintendent Tom Williams to allow two principals to join her for a conference concerning the eight-step process. He agreed and soon found himself with two additional enthusiasts. Franklin and Madison elementary principals helped to conduct meetings to promote the idea to teachers and other administrators, make a plan, and within a year, implement simultaneously at all elementary and middle schools. And though Evans had included the high school in initial meetings, that effort floundered. "We wanted the high school to participate, but due to structural issues and possibly lack of readiness, the beginning effort failed," said Evans.

An on-site representative from the Mississippi Bend Area Education Agency, Don Frost, was assigned to Muscatine High School. His role is to help facilitate the implementation of the eight-step process.

Elementary and middle school teachers and students worked hard to improve 2002 to 2003 math and reading scores by conducting focus lessons in math and reading. They made a significant impact on reading proficiency by combining instructional, focus lessons with SuccessMaker software, a computerized reading program that administers regular quizzes.

Importantly, teachers, administrators, and other staff mentors worked with each individual. With more than one-third of the district school population falling into the lower socioeconomic rank (defined as eligible for free or reduced lunches)—and soaring as high as 64 percent at one elementary—and with many students coming from homes where English is the second language, lower scores had often been excused and accepted. Taking it to a personal level and demonstrating that every child could learn challenged that old culture.

First-year gains for elementary and middle school students brought great pride and accolades. Students increased performance across the board, even closing achievement gaps among socioeconomic groups, while high school performance remained stagnant or declined.

Showcasing the district's efforts, *Time* featured Franklin Elementary's success in a March 2004 article. Pulling itself off the No Child Left Behind act's much-feared "schools in need of improvement" list, Franklin posted a 16 percent gain in reading proficiency and a 28 percent improvement in math. The district was also named a "Gold Medal School District Winner" by Expansion Management, a business publication, and included on its list of "Best Public Schools."

Commitment

When Evans shared the elementary and middle schools' phenomenal success with the district's school board, the members immediately asked why the eight-step process had not been implemented at the high school. She credits the board for getting her "foot in the door"—a door that was soon kicked wide open by a combined, expansive effort: the board, superintendent, high school administrators, teachers, students, parents, and community and business partners.

The elementary and middle school success stories resounded with the 1,600-student high school (the tenth largest in Iowa), despite its unique culture. Even better, the timing proved a windfall. Muscatine High had just received a comprehensive school reform demonstration grant that amounted to $75,000 annually for three years. Thus, the school now had not only the impetus for change, but also the financial resources.

Resources were top of mind when Evans set out the second time to implement the eight-step process at Muscatine High. She was determined to use a proven governance structure: teachers would own the process, and curriculum leaders (formerly referred to as "department heads") would act as the instructional leaders for their topical areas.

"Schools may be tempted to let just anyone volunteer, but I think the way you implement something in a high school—at least this was true in our high school—is through the curriculum departments," said Evans. Curriculum leaders are the most knowledgeable about the subject area, have the most ownership, can develop the lessons, will make sure it is done accurately, and have the leadership to make sure it gets implemented and monitored.

Muscatine High School Administrator Mary Wildermuth, who became the point person responsible for facilitating and acting as liaison between Evans's district role and the teachers on the front line, said this structure and a limited scope were crucial to making giant strides. "In a large high school, we felt we needed to focus on the people we thought would be successful—those who could really pull this off," said Wildermuth.

They focused on math, language arts, and the science departments, as well as the special education teachers in those departments. This allowed the high schools to zoom in on the select few who could get the biggest bang for the initial investment: write the focus lessons, implement them, and quickly demonstrate that success similar to other district schools could also be realized at Muscatine High School.

The acting principal set the expectation and served as cheerleader in supporting the staff's efforts. Wildermuth said this approach was encouraging—like a learning community rather than an authoritative hammer. "We have tried to stay away from punitive action. People are complying because they want this process to happen."

Launch

With curriculum leaders newly charged in June and prepared to work the summer, Pat Davenport made eight-step process presentations and consulted with the math, language arts, and science teams to analyze data, align results with the voluntary state test Iowa Test of Educational Development (ITED) concepts, and begin instructional focus lessons and assessment design. Wildermuth's role was to gather people, make a schedule, facilitate meetings, and most importantly, find resources. "The secret to our success is that we got people the resources they needed," said Wildermuth. "We've put a lot of money into writing the focus lessons and supporting the teachers. That helps with successful implementation."

The most important resource, according to Evans, was time. When Evans and Davenport first presented other school results and talked about the eight-step process, one of the first questions high school teachers asked was, "How do we get the time to meet with all the teachers to plan and collaborate?" The answer was Monday early dismissals. Said Evans, "That time was like gold. I don't think we would have been able to pull all this off if we didn't have that steady, consistent quality staff development time every week." That time did not cost much—just board and community willingness to allow the high school to dismiss students one hour early on Mondays in order to capture this critical preparation and planning period.

Two-hour in-service sessions on Monday afternoons were spent training, collaborating, developing focus lessons and assessments, and developing skills needed to meet one-on-one with students. Training ensured that a skill such as mentoring, which is important to changing the culture, would not be introduced with little guidance. Instead, an in-service was devoted to walking through a "test talk," a mentor-student meeting to discuss ITED, using a student's individual performance profile. The assistant principal and head guidance counselor used overheads, role-playing, and a sample script that emphasized the caring and nurturing skills needed during personal interaction with students.

Teams included every teacher in the three departments as well as AEA staff members and special education teachers. Muscatine has more team-taught classes, in which special education join mainstream classroom teachers, than any other Iowa high school; thus, special education teachers were integral team members who helped design and implement focus lessons.

Although the teams had the detailed data necessary, some language arts and science teachers were uncomfortable inventing focus lessons in the first, time-pressured round of drafts. So Wildermuth acquired workbooks, and Davenport supplied other districts' examples to provide structure and confidence. "If they have a launching pad, then they can go," said Wildermuth.

Mathematics Curricular Leader and Teacher Jean Andres and her math team had an advantage. Using an effective schools grant, they had been analyzing data and searching for ways to improve student achievement prior to this initiative. The department had focused on ITED data, identified the weakest skills, created review worksheets, and concentrated on those skills eight or nine weeks prior to the ITED. Although that process was not tightly structured—Andres said she was unsure whether "every teacher was doing this in every class level"—math scores had shown improvement. But, Andres said, "When we got serious about this eight-step process, we got everybody on board doing the same thing."

Once the new school year began, Davenport again met individually with the three teams leading the change. She also presented the process to an all-staff in-service in an effort to get everyone moving toward a whole-school model. Other teachers began voluntarily participating in integrating lessons that started with simple concepts they were already teaching; the school made clear, however, that all teachers were required to achieve integrated weekly focus lessons by December. Importantly, teachers were expected to begin unifying the message and engaging students.

With Andres' prior achievement efforts, leadership, and renewed emphasis through the eight-step process, the math department became the natural front-runner. They crafted their own focus lessons and assessments. They modified the eight-step process where necessary, such as teaching focus lessons as needed depending on the level of skill in each class, rather than as a daily requirement. Special education teachers also taught the same focus lessons, which Andres said resulted in "everyone on board doing what they needed to do in grades 9, 10, and 11."

Unlike language arts and science, which taught focus lessons but did not administer assessments prior to ITED, the math department's previous efforts helped it to accomplish both. Using assessment results, Andres and her staff reviewed questions to not only determine whether focus lessons were making a difference, but also question validity, potential curriculum gaps from previous years, and teaching performance (i.e., whether the whole department did a good job of teaching the lesson).

Although the departments worked in parallel by focusing solely on their respective departments and spending a tremendous amount of time preparing and writing, Evans and Wildermuth, along with AEA educational consultant Don Frost, served as informal bearers of best practices to increase efficiency and smooth the process.

Revolution

High school staff knew their toughest challenge was finding the right way to engage students. They wanted to connect with each individual and help every student understand the importance of tests, how to approach the tests, and what could be done to improve

performance. They accomplished this through:
- leveraging mentor group bonds,
- engaging students in test talks, and
- borrowing an idea from sports to generate enthusiasm via a pep rally.

Wildermuth said the Muscatine High School mentor program, a "learning community program," had a tremendous impact on making the connection with students and changing culture and climate. This three-year-old program was established to encourage a small, caring group to bond with each other, feel comfortable seeking out the adult leader to assist with questions and problems, and know at least these peers and adult care.

Mentor groups are randomly selected and include three to five students per grade level who remain in the group for the high school duration; graduating seniors are rotated off and replaced with incoming freshmen. Each group is assigned to a teacher, administrator, or counselor. They meet weekly for 20 minutes; Andres emphasized this time is not "a class." In fact, though past meetings included such topics as registration, college scholarship information, grades, and ITED test schedules, the emphasis was team-building initiatives such as community activities (e.g., Toys For Tots at Christmas), board games, and other fun ways to get kids interacting with each other and sharing advice.

The mentoring program idea originated in the district's school improvement advisory committee, which is composed of teachers, administrators, parents, and students who meet bimonthly to discuss student achievement, school-to-work, and communication efforts. Two of the committee's teacher members researched and planned the program, took ownership, and gathered feedback from teachers and students (who have given positive remarks) to refine.

To help ensure success, the program was designed to require minimal planning and preparation effort from teachers. The program leaders plan weekly activities, acquire materials for teachers, and place information on a Web site for teachers to easily download. They are planning a four-year program to ensure students experience something different each year they are involved.

Mentors proved valuable for ITED results. When a high school student suggested high school test scores had not been improving because students never see test results, Evans quickly jumped on the opportunity. She ordered extra individual performance profiles and asked mentors to review with every child in their groups. Through this, the idea of test talks, or individualized attention before and after ITED, was born at Muscatine High School. For those mentors who could not logistically work every child into the schedule, other teachers—and even the superintendent—volunteered to fill in.

Mentors conducted test talks from September until the week prior to the November ITED, usually by carving time from teacher preparation periods. Other teachers accepted a mentor's request that the student be excused from class to attend the test talk. This one-on-one conversation covered all curricular areas, not just that of the mentor, and included discussions regarding how the student could improve in each subject area.

Mentors closed the test talk loop by scheduling individual sessions after the ITED to compare latest to previous results and focus on growth, encouragement, and setting new goals. Mentors encouraged students to discuss their test approach and how they felt about the test. Upon completion of each session, mentors celebrated results by giving students a candy bar specially wrapped and emblazoned with "Thank you for your participation. We appreciate it."

Evans and Andres agree: test talks made a dramatic difference. Andres said, "There has been a lot of interpersonal time between students and teachers that never existed before. That has been a big part of our success." It demonstrated a change in belief. "For so long, students thought the ITED tests meant nothing, that nobody cared. I'm ashamed to say that, for a while there, kids didn't even see their scores because they were left in boxes because it took so long to get results. Depending on whether parents requested them, the results may not even have been sent home."

Teachers had previously only reminded students of upcoming tests, urged them to get a good night's rest and avoid sugary breakfasts, and encouraged them to attend. The new interpersonal approach energized a heartfelt effort to erase the apathy and make each child understand the importance of tests. "We've tried very hard to make kids understand there is a reason for taking these tests," said Andres. "This not only reflects on you, the school, and your community, but also prepares you for your future."

The school's most important goal, Andres said, was helping students understand the link among ITED scores, student futures, and Muscatine's performance as a "good" high school, as well as the broader message that each student counts. "My department took it upon themselves to be excited about 'Let's all improve; let's not just look at the top enriched classes and expect those kids to carry the good scores and too bad about the rest of the kids,'" said Andres. They set a goal to raise one student sub-group by 10 percent and met that goal by paying attention to all kids.

"It's not that we had not paid attention to these kids before; but in teaching, it is very easy to let a low-performing student who does not attend class fall through the cracks," said Andres. "We decided we weren't going to do that any more, and the kids understood that."

Another significant effort increased student scores. When teachers compared ITED and the curriculum, they discovered a discrepancy that was costing students vital points: the high school curriculum did not include "refreshers" for those skills learned in previous grades. Thus, teachers aligned their curricula and increased student preparedness by including refresher topics in focus lessons.

Refreshers and improved test-taking skills gave students more confidence. Andres said that once refresher skills were explained in a new light, students understood these skills were necessary in any grade level of math. They had once known but had since forgotten these basics (e.g., how to select a graph and how to calculate a percentage). And, because many ITED questions address "How do you get the answer?" rather than "Find the answer," teachers worked with students to think more about the process. Other test-taking strategies, such as attempting to answer all questions, were also addressed.

The theme that began as a soft drumbeat in test talks and then increased in decibel during classroom focus lessons, ended in a loud crescendo: the ITED pep rally. "This is the first time in the 30 years I have been at Muscatine that we've had a pep rally or all-school assembly at the high school for the purpose of boosting academic achievement," said Evans. "This was amazing to kids and staff members alike." Similar to a homecoming week pep rally, cheerleaders were on the floor, skits were acted out, and comedic interviews elicited cheers. But the subject was ITED.

Evans acted as "Jane Leno" and conducted "celebrity" interviews. "Mr. Proficiency," a popular math teacher wearing a "41" jersey to remind students that ITED requires a score of at least 41 percentile for "proficiency," challenged students to exceed the cutoff score; "Mr. Prepared," a popular business teacher (and wrestling coach) in suit and tie, complete with his briefcase and sharpened pencils, charged students to get eight hours sleep, eat a healthy breakfast, and have a positive mental attitude. Evans said students saw classmates and faculty alike espousing the benefits of ITED and "acting a little crazy just to get the point across."

The crowd had a particularly inspiring and fun time during the spirited rendition of the Village People's "YMCA" using "I-T-E-D" lyrics distributed beforehand. Andres said the kids seemed shocked to see adults "rocking and having the time of their lives." The pep rally was such a hit that other district schools adopted the idea. "This pep rally was really monumental in changing the culture," said Evans. "I've never seen such excitement and enthusiasm about academics."

Gains

The commitment and enthusiasm paid off. For the short five months its teachers had committed to the eight-step process and the two months spent building stronger connections with students in test talks, Muscatine High significantly improved achievement scores. In math, students increased proficiency by an average of 10 percent (Figure 22, page 174). Likewise, reading proficiency improved by an average of 9 percent.

In its annual improvement goals and report card to stakeholders, the Muscatine Community School District declared its continued commitment to improvement through a focus on student achievement in reading comprehension, math, and science.

Muscatine High School Achievement Scores
2002-2003

Percentage Proficient in Math
2002-2003

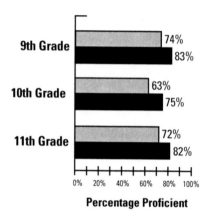

■ 2002
■ 2003

Percentage Proficient in Reading
2002-2003

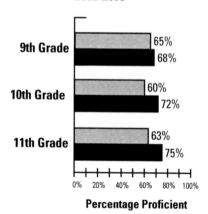

■ 2002
■ 2003

Figure 22

Evolution

Once Muscatine High School showed results, the few remaining stragglers jumped on board. "Even after test talks and the ITED rally, I think there might have been a few teachers who had doubts and didn't really think all kids could learn and improve their scores," said Evans. "When it did happen—and it happened so dramatically—I think they realized we are on to something." That amplified the need to connect by encouraging all teachers, from foreign language to agriculture, to find a way to integrate focus lessons across the school.

Evans began spending the two-hour Monday in-service sessions with teachers of all subject areas, who had become more involved and active in improving achievement. At a recent in-service discussing how to close the socioeconomic and racial gaps, the industrial technology and art teachers proved they were part of the new culture. They advocated smaller class sizes now—not next year—to help English Language Learner students improve reading proficiency. "The sense of urgency is there with all teachers in the high school," said Evans.

While math, language arts, and science refined their work, other leaders took up the cause. Social studies' instructional leader developed an "Essential Social Studies" course designed to provide a strong base in that subject while also integrating crossover skills from ITED tests such as making inferences, looking for supporting details, reviewing maps, and designing charts and graphs. Such cooperation by other departments emphasized and reinforced the instructional focus concepts, said Evans, and contributed to the changing culture.

With proof that their efforts made a meaningful difference in the November ITED scores, language arts and science teachers have "really taken off," said Evans. Although they originally used others' templates to craft focus lessons, they began critiquing and customizing these lessons and writing assessments. They designed a spring 2004 experimental class, which requires parental permission for enrollment, for low-scoring readers who need an intensive focus on specific skills. The student-teacher ratio is small (e.g., 6:1), and the class is offered as a six-week replacement for language arts—thus avoiding duplication and any "punitive" perception.

The math department also continued to review its focus lessons and assessments, which is a process Andres said her staff will continue to do into the future because "We feel like it is effective in the long run to review all lessons and constantly review all steps." Because many ITED skills are basic and not those on which upper-level high school classes focus, these reviews serve as refreshers; the challenge for educators, said Andres, is balancing reviews with necessary new content.

As part of its review and revise process, the math department plans to adapt focus lessons mid year using the latest test data. For example, following the November ITED, focus lessons in math are still based on year-old data; but by spring, they will be replaced with focus lessons targeted at the latest test results. Andres said teachers will use these revised lessons and assessments to jumpstart students' preparation and understanding for the following year's test. Thus, during the spring, eighth-graders will receive ninth-grade focus lessons and assessments that target the weakest skills (those which received the lowest ITED scores) identified in the last test's ninth-grade data; students will be immersed in these skills during the spring and in the last few weeks prior to the November test. The stronger skills (those skills that received the highest ITED scores) will be sandwiched in between, taught at the beginning of the next school year. A similar plan applies across the respective grade levels. (Figure 23 provides a sample 2004 plan.)

	Current 8th Graders	Current 9th Graders	Current 10th Graders
Spring 2004	9th weakest skills	10th weakest skills	11th weakest skills
	9th Graders	**10th Graders**	**11th Graders**
August to September 2004	9th stronger skills	10th stronger skills	11th stronger skills
October 2004	9th weakest skills	10th weakest skills	11th weakest skills
November 2004	9th grade ITED	10th grade ITED	11th grade ITED

Figure 23

Andres said by getting the ideas in students' heads early—especially the lowest-performing skills—and reminding them again in the fall, math teachers hope to produce an even greater performance increase.

Teachers provide tutoring in the classroom setting based on individual need. One approach they found helpful was pairing higher-performing students with those who needed assistance; Andres said peers often provide another perspective or explanation that help students grasp concepts.

The math department plans to tackle another challenge critical to students' success in life: learning basic skills earlier. Andres said she hopes to work with seventh- and eighth-grade teachers next year to compare each level's scores, identify curriculum gaps, and propose lower-level curriculum modifications. She foresees an eventual integration across all grade levels.

Ripples Beyond Muscatine

At the same time Muscatine High acted on the eight-step process, the good news was spreading fast among other schools within the greater Mississippi Bend Area Education Agency. Covering 56,000 students in 43 schools, Mississippi Bend is one of 15 educational agencies in the state that provides resources to individual school districts and help share best practices. Muscatine Community Public Schools sent shockwaves across this network.

Mississippi Bend AEA Curriculum and School Improvement Consultant Mary Beilke said several AEA schools have begun the eight-step process as the result of Muscatine's success. Recently, an additional 14 schools have voluntarily started the process. Like administrators at individual schools, the AEA encourages ownership at the lowest level and thus acts as a consultant and facilitator; its role is providing resources, encouragement, and guidance.

Although Iowa does not have state-adopted standards and instead leaves these standards for schools to define, a "local control" required by Iowa law, Beilke said most schools have similar standards that are typically more comprehensive than the state-tested basic skills. Her agency offers a list of best-practice standards as well as training, a staff development Web site, a listserv that fans information to buildings, and workshops as requested; the agency is considering a best practices repository for the near future.

Beilke and other Mississippi Bend AEA professional development consultants help review data and identify weaknesses, but she emphasized that each school makes its own decisions on how to govern and implement the process. "This is their data for their kids that they know," said Beilke. She said the key is tailoring the eight-step process to the unique needs of each school's students and remaining flexible to those changing needs.

Important to this process, said Beilke, is understanding it focuses on continuous improvement rather than just a one-time, purchase-and-install program. It focuses instructional decision making and helps students understand and accept that "measurement is a part of our lives," whether in academic tests, college entrance exams, or employer performance evaluations. Beilke urges school leaders to clarify that the intent of the eight-step process is to measure system performance rather than student potential.

Success Factors

Muscatine High School's success has become a role model for not only Mississippi Bend AEA, but also Iowa and beyond. Teachers, professional development groups, and others interested in sharing best practices have asked high school leaders to share their experiences. When asked to distill critical success factors from their observations, Wildermuth, Evans, and Andres reiterate four practices:
1. teacher ownership and commitment,
2. a manageable scope,
3. customized materials focused on students' specific needs, and
4. student connection.

First, these three leaders who helped transform Muscatine High School agreed, the wave of change begins with fully engaged and enthusiastic leaders. Administration support and guidance are important; but for the daily implementation on the front line, instructional leadership and teacher commitment are indispensable.

The teachers possess the expertise, classroom touch, and knowledge of individual students.

Enabling teacher success, however, requires a focused rollout that is manageable in size. "If you try to do too many things and have too many agendas, you won't accomplish your goals," said Wildermuth. "In in-service, we kept the main thing the main thing, rather than having an outside speaker come in and talk about something extraneous."

Although packaged materials helped staff in a time crunch, Andres said customized materials, based on individual school data, make the biggest difference. By reviewing school data, Andres and her staff found the same curriculum gaps for the previous five years of testing. They targeted focus lessons and assessments to close those gaps and hope future integration with elementary and middle school focus lessons and assessments will identify and eliminate those gaps earlier.

The best leadership and curriculum integration will matter little if high school students don't "buy it"—a rather tricky matter, said Andres. "Truly, it is difficult to convince high school kids that they need math and reading skills to be successful in today's society." Far better than "telling them," which can often only incite rebellion, Muscatine High tried "a gentle shove in the right direction," said Andres.

They set out to change much more than test scores. One by one, teachers and administrators deepened bonds with students, demonstrated the school's commitment to making a difference in each of their lives, and persistently uprooted old, demoralizing beliefs. And although there is no magic formula to bottle and toss at-sea for the multitude of schools anxious to make waves of their own, this high school's message proved plenty potent.

About the
American Productivity & Quality Center

A n internationally recognized resource for process and
performance improvement, the American Productivity &
Quality Center (APQC) helps organizations adapt to rapidly
changing environments, build new and better ways to work,
and succeed in a competitive marketplace. With a focus on
benchmarking, knowledge management, metrics, performance
measurement, and quality improvement initiatives, APQC works
with its member organizations to identify best practices, discover
effective methods of improvement, broadly disseminate findings,
and connect individuals with one another and the knowledge,
training, and tools they need to succeed. Founded in 1977, APQC is
a member-based nonprofit serving organizations around the world in
all sectors of business, education, and government.

Today, APQC works with organizations across all industries
to find practical, cost-effective solutions to drive productivity and
quality improvement. APQC offers a variety of products and services
including:
- consortium, custom, and metric benchmarking studies;
- publications, including books, Best-practice Reports, and
  implementation guides;
- computer-based, on-site, and custom training;
- consulting and facilitation services; and
- networking opportunities.

PUBLICATIONS

APQC is the preeminent source for leading-edge organizational
research and improvement information. Designed to ease your way
to positive results, APQC publications come in many forms and
cover a wide range of subjects. APQC has a number of publications
created specifically for educators that are focused on using

data-driven instructional tools and strategies to improve student and system performance. Popular titles from APQC's quickly expanding publications catalog include:

- *A Guide to Reinventing Schools* by RISC
- *Benchmarking Best Practices in Accountability Systems in Education*
- *Benchmarking in Education: Pure & Simple*
- *Closing the Achievement Gap: No Excuses* by Gerald Anderson and Patricia Davenport
- *Continuous Improvement Tools in Education: Volume 1*
- *Continuous Improvement Tools in Education: Volume 2*
- *Disaggregating Data in Schools: Leveraging the Information You Have*
- *Educators in Action: Examining Strategic Improvement Efforts*
- *Improving Teacher Education and Preparation*
- *PDCA Instructional Cycle*
- *Solving Problems in Schools: A Guide for Educators* by Paige Leavitt
- *Today's Teaching and Learning: Leveraging Technology*

These and other titles can be ordered through APQC's online bookstore at www.apqc.org/pubs.

Additional Resources

Edvance

Edvance is a nonprofit organization dedicated to improving student achievement by helping educational organizations advance good ideas to sustainable implementation with measurable results. It combines established methodologies for benchmarking effective practices with innovative technology and services to complete the path from idea to effective implementation. As a conglomeration of the Education Initiative at the American Productivity and Quality Center and individuals who worked for the technology team at the University of Texas Center for Reading and Language Arts, Edvance staff have diverse backgrounds in business and academia. By maintaining close relationships with research one universities and APQC, Edvance balances academic development and improvement with business-like requirements for quality, efficiency, customer satisfaction and accountability.

info@edvance.org
866-EDVANCE (1-866-338-2623)

Training

Patricia Davenport
Equity in Education
pdavenport@equityineducation.com
832-721-6202

Gerald E. Anderson
Equity, Excellence & Quality Center
eeqc@earthlink.net
979-299-5572